David Hume

NICHOLAS PHILLIPSON

David Hume

The Philosopher as Historian

Yale

UNIVERSITY PRESS

New Haven & London

This revised edition first published in the United States in 2012 by Yale University Press.
This revised edition first published in Great Britain in 2011 by Penguin Books.
First published as *Hume* by Weidenfeld & Nicolson 1989.

Yale University Press books may be purchased in quantity for educational,
business, or promotional use. For information, please e-mail sales.press@yale.edu
(U.S. office) or sales@yaleup.co.uk (U.K. office).

Set in 9.25/12.5 pt. Sabon LT Std.
Typeset by Palimpsest Book Production Limited, Falkirk, Stirlingshire.

Printed in the United States of America.

A catalogue record for this book is available from the British Library.
Library of Congress Control Number: 2011940745
ISBN 978-0-300-18166-1 (pbk.)

10 9 8 7 6 5 4 3 2 1

Contents

Author's Note

This book was originally published in 1989 as a contribution to *Historians on Historians*, a series of short books by historians writing about their favourite historians. This excellent project, which was the brainchild of Juliet Gardiner, was aborted by the publisher shortly after its launch, and it deserves to be relaunched. *David Hume: The Philosopher as Historian* is a slightly extended and amended version of the original edition, the approach and the line of argument remaining the same.

Nicholas Phillipson
Edinburgh, November 2010

Chronology

Prologue

David Hume's reputation has never been higher. In the eyes of many philosophers, he is the prophet of the Wittgensteinian revolution that has helped to shape our understanding of human knowledge and of the nature of philosophy itself. By insisting that it is the task of the philosopher to attend to the beliefs we hold about the world and the language in which they are expressed, Hume, like his modern disciples, appears as a philosopher who paved the way for an anthropologically based understanding of the belief-systems which make society coherent and human behaviour intelligible. In the eyes of many historians, too, Hume is a prophet of modernity. For he was that most remarkable of eighteenth-century oddities, an untroubled religious sceptic who declared war on Christianity by showing that an unbeliever who reflected carefully and systematically on human behaviour as it was evidenced in ordinary life could produce a far more closely textured and coherent account of the principles of human nature than theologians or Christian philosophers. He did so in the belief that it was better to teach human beings to gear their lives to the pursuit of happiness in the world of common life than to pursue the uncertain and imaginary joys of happiness in a life hereafter. As he once asked a Christian friend, 'For pray, what is the End of Man? Is he created for Happiness or for Virtue? For this Life or for the next? For himself or for his Maker?'[1]

Such views are fine, so far as they go. But they give rise to a curious paradox. Modern enthusiasm for Hume is derived, in the last resort, from our admiration for a book which few of Hume's contemporaries read and fewer understood, a book which would ultimately be disowned by its author in the most unequivocal terms. This book was *A Treatise of Human Nature* (1739–40). It was here that Hume tackled the formidable problem of disentangling the study of human behaviour from the theological assumptions in which it had become enmeshed; here that he set out the principles on which a genuinely secular, genuinely empirical investigation could be carried out. No one doubts that the *Treatise* contains the building blocks on which all his subsequent writing was based. No one doubts – and nor did Hume – that what he accomplished was nothing less than a philosophical revolution. As he wrote in the introduction, 'In pretending . . . to explain the principles of human nature, we in effect propose a compleat system of the sciences, built on a foundation almost entirely new, and the only one upon which they can stand with any security.'[2] On the other hand, he was crestfallen by the book's reception; while it did not exactly fall 'stillborn from the press' as he claimed, it certainly did not reach the popular readership that he had hoped for.

So he turned his insatiable curiosity about human behaviour from the general to the particular and to the politics and culture of contemporary Britain, whose free constitution and thriving commerce was becoming the envy of the civilized world. It was to be an exercise in using his metaphysical discoveries about the way in which human beings try to make sense of the world, to throw light on the way in which modern Britons tried to make sense of the political life of Walpolian Britain. He did this in a series of polite, popular essays, published in 1741, 1742 and 1747, which were written for readers of the periodical press and those who had been brought up on popular moral and political reviews like the *Spectator* and the *Craftsman*. These *Essays Moral, Political and Literary* did not sell well either. Having again failed to find a public for his philosophy, he tried a third time and wrote sophisticated and elegant accounts of his metaphysical, moral and political philosophy to explain the general principles of his analysis of modern British politics to the ordinary, educated reader. These were contained in his *Enquiry Concerning Human Understanding* (1748), the *Enquiry Concerning the Principles of Morals* (1751) and the *Political Discourses* (1752). But only the last, which dealt with the political management of a polity which was being transformed by commerce, attracted much public attention. Indeed, by the end of the decade it had established itself at home and abroad as one of the foundation stones of the new and increasingly influential science of political economy, a status it has enjoyed from that day to this.

By 1760, however, Hume's fortunes were changing dramatically. In the late 1740s he had decided to embark on a history of Great Britain, which would explain the origins of the political system he had analysed in his *Essays* and would replace the histories on which party politicians relied for their polemics. This vast work, more than a million words long, occupied nearly fifteen years of Hume's life and appeared in six volumes between 1754 and 1762. It was as devastating, intellectually, as the *Treatise*. It was designed to encourage modern Britons to think about the stories they had been told about the history of civilization in their country, to ask whether there were not better ways of explaining it than those of the party hacks, and to reflect on the disastrous political misunderstandings that could arise when political opinions were corrupted by an inadequate understanding of history. This history reached the popular audience Hume had always longed for and gingered up the market for all his earlier works except the *Treatise*. For that 'juvenile work', which 'the Author had projected before he left College, . . . which he wrote and published not long after' and which has been in print continuously for more than a century; that work which has become part of the furniture of our philosophical thinking and remains one of the cornerstones of the philosophical curricula of Anglo-Saxon universities; that work was written off as premature. 'I have repented my Haste [in publishing it] a hundred, & a hundred times.'[3] On the other hand, the *History of England* which established Hume's intellectual reputation and was the most important contemporary vehicle for his thought, is now all but ignored by philosophers and historians and was out of print from 1894 until it was republished by an enterprising specialist publisher in 1983. As a result, Hume the historian has been forgotten and, more importantly, the profoundly historical content of his philosophy has been overlooked.

And that is what this short book is about. I want to present Hume as the most historically minded of philosophers and the most subtly and profoundly philosophical of historians, a thinker whose mastery of the metaphysical facts of human life was matched only by his mastery of British historiography. No other philosopher has developed an understanding of human nature which has been able to sustain so meticulously detailed an analysis of political events as Hume. Nor has any other historian been guided by a philosophy which is as nuanced and profound as Hume's; here Marx and Collingwood are surely his only rivals. This book is also about a philosophical historian, or a historian–philosopher, it doesn't matter which, who not only believed that philosophy and history were of importance in public life but who showed *why* they were so and *how* exactly philosophical and historical understanding could help to reshape the behaviour of ordinary, literate men and women. It also traces the step-by-step progress by which one of the greatest of Western philosophers turned himself into one of the greatest historians of Britain, a progress that was entirely natural and awesome in its demands on a remarkable intellect. Finally, it offers enough of a taste of the contents of the *History of England* to whet the appetites of those who admire precision and intelligence in historical thinking. For that is what is on offer in abundance in this neglected masterpiece of British historical writing.

I

Life and Letters

David Hume was born on 26 April 1711. He was the son of a fairly typical family of Scottish border gentry. The Humes of Ninewells were a well-established Berwickshire family of strict Presbyterians, who were reasonably well off by Scottish standards and had long been accustomed to play a full part in local affairs. Hume's father died suddenly in 1713, leaving his widow with a pile of debts and three children to bring up. Katherine Hume came from a distinguished legal family and, while she had no intellectual pretensions whatever, she was a kind, sensible, devout woman who devoted the rest of her life to a family which always remained closely and affectionately knit. Indeed, Hume's family correspondence strongly suggests that, younger son though he was, he became the mainstay of his family after her death.

Like his father, grandfather and any intelligent boy of his class, Hume was destined for the law, then as now the classic gateway to a career in Scottish public life. He must have been a precocious child, because he was sent to Edinburgh University in 1723 with his elder brother at the unusually early age of twelve; fourteen would have been more normal. There, he recalled, 'I passed through the ordinary course of education with success,' taking the usual diet of Latin, Greek, Logic and Metaphysics, and Natural Philosophy which was later spiced up with courses in mathematics and probably civil history. He then passed on to the dreary routines of legal education during which 'I found an insurmountable Aversion to every thing but the pursuits of Philosophy and general Learning; and while [my family] fanceyed I was poring over Voet and Vinnius, Cicero and Vergil were the Authors which I was secretly devouring.'[1]

Hume left university with a singular lack of enthusiasm for professors. 'As you know,' he told a friend in 1735, 'there is nothing to be learned from a Professor, which is not to be met with in Books.'[2] On the other hand, his arrival in Edinburgh could not have happened at a more important period in the city's history. The Anglo-Scottish Union of 1707 had absorbed the Scottish political system into that of an English, or, as some preferred to call it, a British state. It had led to the dismantling of the Scots' Parliament and Privy Council, to the exodus of the notoriously factious and venal Scottish nobility to London, and to the dislocation of the retail trade, the social life and the prestige of Edinburgh, which became what one Victorian described, melodramatically, as a 'widowed metropolis'.[3] This was something of an exaggeration. After the Union Edinburgh still housed the General Assembly of the Church of Scotland and the Court of Session and remained the centre of the country's religious and legal life. It also housed the country's banks and tax offices. By Hume's day, it had acquired a new lease of political life. The Earl of Islay, later the 3rd Duke of Argyll, had been placed in charge of the political management of Scotland and was being described as the 'uncrowned king of Scotland', a reputation he enjoyed almost uninterrupted until his death in 1761. Under his governance Edinburgh once more became the focal point of Scottish public life. Informally, at least, it was not unlike Dublin, Boston or Charleston, the capital city of one of the great provinces of the British Crown.

Hume was the most gregarious of men, well aware of the cultural changes which were taking place in Edinburgh in the 1720s. For the city was becoming the centre of a remarkable experiment in rebuilding the country's political and religious culture. The lengthy debates about the state of contemporary Scotland which had preceded the Act of Union had alerted the Scots to the problems of a small country with a defective constitution and an underdeveloped economy. The Union had been an attempt to solve its constitutional and economic problems. By Hume's day, the lairds, lawyers, doctors, clergy, professors and wits of Edinburgh had begun to tackle its cultural problems. The city's taverns, coffee-houses and salons had begun to generate a sophisticated club culture, which was designed to show how learning and letters could help to eradicate religious and political faction, encourage the spread of politeness and perform the patriotic task of civilizing the country and strengthening its 'independence'. The university too had been radically restructured in the early years of the Union, in order to make it attractive to gentlemen as well as the Kirk and to train up lawyers and doctors as well as ministers and parish schoolmasters. By 1723, the year in which Hume went to university, one local citizen could write optimistically,

> It is . . . well known, That the City of Edinburgh, is, at present, a Place which excels in the Means of a virtuous and liberal Education, and wherein all the Parts of Learning are taught to great Perfection, by Gentlemen of great Abilities, Sufficiency and Diligence; and that there may be great Proficiency made by Youth, in the Studies of Divinity, Law, Philosophy in all the Parts of it, History, Ecclesiastical and Civil, Physick, Anatomy and Musick, as also, the different Languages and exactly taught.[4]

Hume spent many of his formative years in a city which was deeply preoccupied with this sort of *perestroika* and would become a leading member of a *literati* which thought of the preservation of Scottish independence in terms of the improvement of its constitution, its commerce and its culture.

In 1729, when he was eighteen, Hume seems to have made a philosophical discovery of the utmost importance which opened up what he described as 'a new scene of thought'. We cannot be entirely sure what this discovery was, but it seems most likely to have been his theory of causality. It was here that he showed that our ability to understand the causal relations which regulate events in the world and make it possible for us to understand our place in it, was based on sentiment, not reason, and was shaped by experience and history, not by abstract, timeless, general laws. If Hume really *had* succeeded in formulating this theory in 1729, he had already made a discovery which was to have the most profound and disturbing implications for the study of human behaviour. At the same time, he was laying the intellectual foundations of a programme which was to occupy the rest of his life. For the theory of causality made it possible for him not only to *historicize* the study of human behaviour, but to lay the foundations of a new analysis of the history of civilization in Britain which showed how little modern Britons understood of their constitution and their past, and how dangerously ill-equipped they were to preserve liberty and happiness in a modern age.

Hume spent the next decade working intensively on his philosophical masterpiece, *A Treatise of Human Nature* (1739–40). He seems to have spent much of his time in total isolation, conducting thought experiments on himself with the utmost rigour. It was an awesomely taxing psychological experience, doubly so for someone as naturally gregarious as Hume, and it is just possible that it drove him to the edge of a nervous breakdown. In the *Treatise*, he described the experience with some anguish,

> I am first affrighted and confounded with that forlorn solitude, in which I am plac'd in my philosophy, and fancy myself some strange uncouth monster, who not being able to mingle and unite in society, has been expell'd all human commerce, and left utterly abandon'd and disconsolate. Fain wou'd I run into the crowd for shelter and warmth; but cannot prevail with myself to mix with such deformity. I call upon others to join me, in order to make a company apart; but no-one will hearken to me. Every one keeps at a distance, and dreads that storm, which beats upon me from every side.[5]

On learning about these experiments, however, his mother is supposed to have commented, 'Our Davie's a fine good-natur'd cratur, but uncommon weak-minded.'[6]

Hume thought that his *Treatise* had placed the study of human behaviour on 'an entirely new footing', and would be recognized for the revolutionary book it was by ordinary citizens as well as the learned. This was ingenuous. The *Treatise* was and remains long, dense and difficult, and Hume was bitterly disappointed to find that it was little read outside the sophisticated circle of his Scottish friends, on whom it was soon to have a profound influence. But the last chapters of the *Treatise* make it clear that he was already applying his analysis to the problems of contemporary Britain, and writing so that citizens and legislators could apply his philosophy to their own business; it was a project which would occupy him for the rest of his life. In three short, elegant volumes of *Essays Moral and Political*, later retitled *Essays Moral, Political and Literary*, he provided a quite remarkable account of the constitution and political culture of Walpolian Britain and showed how it had developed since the Glorious Revolution. *An Enquiry Concerning Human Understanding, An Enquiry Concerning the Principles of Morals* ('of all my writings, historical, philosophical, or literary, incomparably the best'), the *Political Discourses* and the posthumously published *Dialogues Concerning Natural Religion* (composed around 1751) analysed contemporary discourse about metaphysics, morals, politics and natural religion, and encouraged intelligent citizens to think again about the best ways of pursuing virtue and happiness in a modern commercial polity.

By this time, Hume's work was attracting replies and rebuttals, the *Political Discourses* particularly. As he recalled,

> Mean-while, my Bookseller, A Millar, informed me, that my former Publications (all but the unfortunate Treatise) were beginning to be the Subject of Conversation, that the Sale of them was gradually encreasing, and that new Editions were demanded. Answers, by Reverends and Right Reverends, came out two or three in a Year: And I found by Dr Warburtons Railing, that the Books were beginning to be esteemed in good Company.[7]

Hume's scepticism made conflict with the Church all but inevitable and nowhere more so than in Scotland. It cost him chairs of moral philosophy at Edinburgh and Glasgow – not surprisingly, as the primary purpose of the professor was to teach budding ministers of the Kirk. It also drew him into a highly publicized and acrimonious conflict with the high-flying clergy in the early 1750s, along with his friends and namesakes, Henry Home, the future Lord Kames, and the Rev. John Home, the author of a celebrated and supposedly blasphemous tragedy called *Douglas*. Hume himself was charged with heresy and was successfully defended by his friends among the young moderate clergy on the classic grounds that a non-believer lay outside the jurisdiction of the Church. It was an action which Hume never forgot, for which he was always grateful, and which did something to persuade him that modern religion need not always be sunk in ignorance and bigotry. As he wrote at the end of his life,

> It is happy for the inhabitants of this metropolis [Edinburgh], which has naturally a great influence on the country, that the same persons, who can make such a figure in profane [Hume later substituted 'polite'] learning, are entrusted with the guidance of the people in their spiritual concerns, which are of such superior, and indeed of unspeakable importance! These illustrious examples [he is speaking of the moderate clergy], if any thing, must make the infidel abashed of his vain cavails, and put a stop to that torrent of vice, profaneness, and immorality, by which the age is so unhappily corrupted.[8]

By the 1750s, Hume's philosophy was beginning to fertilize Scottish intellectual culture. Adam Smith – possibly his closest friend and probably the contemporary who understood him best – was incurring important philosophical debts as he developed the remarkable moral philosophy curriculum at Glasgow University out of which *The Wealth of Nations* was to grow. The Aberdonian philosopher Thomas Reid had begun to develop a sophisticated and influential Christian critique of Hume's metaphysics, which was to exert a quite remarkable influence on academic philosophy in Anglo-Saxon and Continental universities at the turn of the eighteenth and nineteenth centuries. The natural philosophers and medical doctors of Edinburgh and Glasgow, too, were beginning to digest the implications of Hume's metaphysics for their own disciplines. Humean scepticism was proving to be a crucial – perhaps *the* crucial – force in shaping the intellectual culture of the Scottish Enlightenment.

But by the early 1750s Hume had already abandoned philosophy and was working on his *History of England*. He had been appointed librarian to the Faculty of Advocates in Edinburgh in 1752. The post gave him control of the finest library in Scotland and the materials he most needed for the early volumes. The first dealt with the reigns of James I and Charles I, the second with the later Stuarts and the Glorious Revolution. The third and fourth dealt with the Tudors and the explosive question of the Reformation. The last two volumes went back to the early history of England and to the Middle Ages. As an unfriendly critic once remarked, like the witches, he had said his prayers backwards.[9]

The *History* was written to a specific agenda which had been developed in earlier philosophical and political writing. Hume's primary purpose was to explain the origins of the modern constitution and the party system. As always, his intentions were critical and revisionist and his history still makes uncomfortable reading. Not only did he show that the origins of the constitution were not in the least ancient, as so many Englishmen fondly believed, but that the party system was an essential and ineradicable part of it. Most disturbing of all, he made a point of showing how the Church had succeeded in corrupting politics at nearly every important period of British history. Overall the history of England as told by Hume could hardly have been less glorious. It was the story of a continuing and often fruitless struggle on the part of a long line of rulers to preserve government from the hands of ambitious and often bigoted usurpers. It was the story of a constitution which had always been, and still remained, in a state of continual flux. It was a story which showed how seldom power had been exercised with wisdom or prudence and how often political opinion had been corrupted by ignorance, superstition and zealotry. And Hume held out only the most cautious hope that the civilizing powers of commerce would be enough to preserve the constitution for the future.

Not surprisingly, the *History* caused a furore. The all-important first volume, which dealt with the early Stuarts,

> was assailed by one Cry of Reproach, Disapprobation, and even Detestation: English, Scotch, and Irish; Whig and Tory; Churchman and Sectary, Free thinker and Religionist; Patriot and Courtier united in their Rage against the Man, who had presumed to shed a generous Tear for the Fate of Charles I, and the Earl of Strafford: And after the first Ebullitions of this Fury were over, what was still more mortifying, the Book seemed to sink into Oblivion.[10]

The reception of the other volumes was not much more friendly. However, the *History* did attract public attention and began to sell well both in Britain and overseas, finally establishing Hume's reputation as an intellectual of the first rank.

By 1762, when the last volume appeared, Hume was in his fifties and ready to settle down. He had never married, and during the 1740s and 1750s had exercised the bachelor's prerogative of living a peripatetic life. He had lived for short periods in London, travelled in France, tutored a madman and spent some time as a diplomat, finding what time he could for writing and frequently returning to his family in Scotland, where he was able to enjoy the sophisticated, gregarious and bucolic intellectual life of enlightened Edinburgh. For then, as always, Hume valued friendship as one of the highest virtues, and conversation and claret as essential to civilized living. And not all the pleasure of being lionized in Paris in 1763 could stop him from admitting that 'I really wish often for the plain roughness of the Poker [Club of Edinburgh] . . . to correct and qualify so much luciousness.'[11]

The success of the *History* made him 'not only independent but opulent', and allowed him to toy with the idea of settling in London. But the Scotophobic zealotry and folly of Londoners disgusted him; the English were, he complained, '[a] Nation . . . relapsing fast into the deepest Stupidity, Christianity & Ignorance'.[12] For a time, he thought of moving to Paris, but that plan too was abandoned. And so, in 1767, he finally decided to settle for the familiar pleasures of Edinburgh, then at the height of its intellectual reputation and populated with a polite patriotic and intelligent laity and a thankfully moderate and learned clergy. And, anyway, where else could a modern pagan's arrival be celebrated with such excellent doggerel as that which appeared on the front page of the *Caledonian Mercury* of 6 September 1769? It is an address 'To D—— H——, Esq; on his return to Edinburgh' and it reads like the work of his friend, the playwright John Home. It ends,

What tho' Londona's over-weening pride,
Fond of her race, and just to few beside,
Refuse the merit Europe's wits proclaim,
And sicken at the sounding of your name;
What tho' barbarians on the banks of Thames,
Their genius sunk in Lucre's sordid flames,

Despise the SCOT, and hate the letter'd sage,
Your name my son, shall stretch from age to age;
Like some great stream, indignant, burst each mound,
While shallow envy prostrate bites the ground.
Let then London a still with greatness dwell,
With Wilkes and Liberty, and Green and Horne,
And P[it]t, and Beck[for]d, ring from morn to morn;
Let patriot-worthies, in her own Guildhall,
Teach Monarchs wisdom, and be all in all:
For joys so turbulent I ne'er shall pine,
Nor e'er shall envy, while a HUME is mine.[13]

Hume spent the last decade of his life in Edinburgh as an hon-
oured and favourite citizen, moving house so that he could live more
comfortably and entertain more generously, taking trouble to keep
good company with the younger *literati* and clergy, to the understandable horror of strict divines. In these last years he seems to have
set out to show a deeply Christian society that a pagan could live
virtuously. By 1773 he had contracted cancer but it was not allowed
to interrupt his literary or social life. He wrote a brief, brilliant essay,
'Of the Origins of Government', to recapitulate and reinforce the
central principles of his political thought and his political teaching.
He made meticulous arrangements to ensure that his *Dialogues Concerning Natural Religion* would be published after his death. He
wrote a short, precise, quietly revealing autobiography, confessing
that 'my love of literary fame', that most pagan of virtues, had always
been his ruling passion. He corrected proofs for a new edition of his
works. And all the time he kept open house to his friends. James
Boswell, morbidly troubled by death as usual, was one of these:
'[Hume] was lean, ghastly, and quite of an unearthly appearance. He
was dressed in a suit of grey cloth with white buttons, and a kind of
scratch wig. He was quite different from the plump figure which he
used to present.' They chatted about religion and Boswell 'had a
strong curiosity to be satisfied if he persisted in disbelieving a future
state even when he had death before his eyes . . . I asked him if it was
not possible that there might be a future state. He answered it was
possible that a piece of coal put upon the fire would not burn; and he

added that it was a most unreasonable fancy that we should exist for ever.' Boswell went on to ask 'if the thought of annihilation never gave him any uneasiness':

> He said not the least; no more than the thought that he had not been, as Lucretius observes. 'Well,' said I, 'Mr. Hume, I hope to triumph over you when I meet you in a future state; and remember you are not to pretend that you was joking with all this infidelity.' 'No, no,' said he. 'But I shall have been so long there before you come that it will be nothing new.' In this style of good humour and levity did I conduct the conversation.

Only once did the mood change: 'He then said flatly that the morality of every religion was bad, and, I really thought, was not jocular when he said that when he heard a man was religious, he concluded he was a rascal, though he had known some instances of very good men being religious.'

Boswell 'left him with impressions which disturbed me for some time'.[14] For Hume had shown him that a pagan could understand the world, live well and die without fear in a manner of which no decent Christian could disapprove.

All of Hume's philosophy, all of his history, was to be directed towards the goal of teaching men and women to seek happiness in the world of common life rather than in the life hereafter, and to pay attention to their duties to their fellow citizens rather than to a suppositious deity. But so far as his readers were concerned, the world of common life was a civilized world, regulated by government, law, religion, commerce and culture. As a philosopher, Hume set out to discover what civilization was, and how it could be cultivated. As a historian, he set out to discover how it had developed in Britain and how it could be preserved and improved in the future. For philosophy and history had taught him that moderns did not understand civilization and that their thought had been seriously damaged by religion. But all Hume's thinking about the history of civilization was to be shaped by his profound belief in the civilizing powers of the commerce which was transforming Western Europe and, so modern Scots hoped, would eventually civilize even Scotland. He was to go out of his way to emphasize the scale of a revolution which was shifting wealth from the nobility to the people, which had created a middling rank of independently minded gentry, professionals and merchants and was increasing the happiness of the poor. But his philosophy and history showed that this revolution would only continue its civilizing course if men and women cultivated more of the worldly values Christianity had traditionally abhorred and if they acquired a better understanding of the political history of their country. Teaching those lessons was the task of the modern man of letters, which Hume viewed with the detachment of the modern Scot and the resources of scepticism and science.

2

Politics, Politeness and
Men of Letters

Hume was to be the philosopher and historian of a volatile and divided nation. The English had executed one king, Charles I, in 1649, less than a century before the publication of the *Treatise* and they had deposed another, James II, as recently as 1688. They had placed a Dutchman on the throne in 1688 and a German, George I, in 1714, shocking supporters of the old Stuart dynasty and ensuring that the future of the monarchy would continue to be insecure during the first half of the eighteenth century. They had experimented with the constitution as well, dabbling with republicanism in the 1650s only to see it degenerate into the military despotism of Oliver Cromwell. In 1688, they had established a 'mixed monarchy', part monarchy, part republic; by Hume's student days, that too had degenerated into a corrupt Whig oligarchy led by Sir Robert Walpole. So far as Hume was concerned, all of this only illustrated what his philosophy and history were to prove, that the crust of civilization was always thin, generally friable and never to be taken for granted. What is more, Britain's dismal recent history simply showed that the English, unlike the Scots, did not have the slightest understanding of their constitution, their commerce or their culture. Indeed they seemed perfectly capable of destroying all three simultaneously.

These apprehensions about the future of civilization in Britain, which helped to make Hume the 'sceptical Whig' he thought himself to be, also made him one of the most formidable analysts of this or any other period of British history, and they remained with him for the rest of his life. By the 1760s, when the *History of England* was complete, he was still convinced that the problem of preserving civilization in England lay in protecting the constitution from the ignorance and folly of a factious people who were only able to rise above their tribal party loyalties when aroused by xenophobia and religion. Indeed, Hume never wavered in his view that it was Britain, not France, that was heading for revolution in the later eighteenth century and it was France, not Britain, that was the very model of a free and civilized monarchy. It is a staggering misjudgement on the part of one of the most acute of all political analysts, which only serves to remind us that his mind was formed in the bleak and turbulent political world of early-eighteenth-century Britain.

Hume was to become an acute and sceptical student of party, a term he used interchangeably with faction and applied to the family feuds that had been endemic in the tiny city-states of the ancient and modern world and the baronial feuds of the Middle Ages, about which he wrote in the last two volumes of the *History of England*.[1] Indeed he was able to show that there was not much to choose between the party politicians of the modern era and the feudal baronage; both had succeeded in destabilizing British society and both had obstructed the progress of civilization as a consequence. But what interested him about the party conflicts of the modern era was that struggles for power between politicians had been shaped and complicated by religious differences and even differences over highly abstract points of political ideology. It was striking, for example, that the opposition to Charles I in England and Scotland had been accompanied by attempts to turn the two kingdoms into godly commonwealths, that opposition to James II had been dictated by fears of popery, that political divisions at Court, in Parliament and in the country were profoundly influenced by divisions within the Church of England and the Church of Scotland about the principles of religion in a Protestant state and about the relationship between the Established Churches and dissenting communities.

These differences had been compounded by ideologies which embodied radically different conceptions of the constitution, something that Hume saw as a dangerous and, indeed, menacing fissure in contemporary political culture. It was generally held that the Glorious Revolution of 1688 had established or restored 'mixed monarchy' in

Britain. The Revolution Settlement had stated the principles of a constitution which was part republican, part monarchical. Political authority had been distributed between king, lords and commons so that, when the constitution was in perfect equilibrium, no single estate would be able to dominate the others. In such a state, so it was believed, liberty, property and religion would be secure. It was a constitution to be admired because it was rational, because it conformed to classical ideals of a free constitution, and because it seemed to restate and perfect the principles of a constitution whose origins were supposed to lie in the gothic past.

Jacobite supporters of the Stuart dynasty, which was finally displaced by the accession of George 1 in 1714, regarded the mixed constitution with dismay. They were committed to beliefs in the divine and absolute rights of monarcy, in the duty of passive obedience on the part of citizens and in the indefeasible rights of the Stuart dynasty. They regarded mixed monarchy as a recipe for political disaster, not least because there were bound to be differences of opinion about the proper balance which ought to exist between its component parts and about those things which seemed to threaten its equilibrium; and these differences could only breed dissension and encourage resistance to established authority. Jacobites concluded that absolute hereditary monarchy was a necessary precondition for political stability and that its authority was sanctioned by experience and religion. Attempts to undermine the indefeasible rights of the Stuart dynasty to the throne threatened not only to turn Britain into an elective monarchy but to open the floodgates to opinion, dissension and what Charles Leslie described as 'The Kingdom of ME'.[2] Such views of divine and indefeasible right had flourished before 1714 and were pushed underground by the defeat of the Jacobite Rebellion of 1715. Nevertheless, as Hume knew well and modern historians have recently confirmed, in spite of the increasingly tight oligarchic grip which Walpole's Whig junto exerted on the political nation after 1715, Britain remained at grass roots a deeply xenophobic nation, resentful of foreign kings, Whig corruption, papists and dissenters and it continued to be doggedly, if largely passively, loyal to the Stuarts, to the supremacy of the Church of England and to traditional views of divine right.[3]

As we shall see, these beliefs were part of a political culture which acquired its most developed historiographical expression in 1747, in the Jacobite antiquary Thomas Carte's gigantic history of England, which appeared just as Hume's attention was turning from contemporary politics to history.

When Hume analysed the politics of Walpolian Britain in 1741 in his *Essays Moral and Political*, he did so as one who believed that the Glorious Revolution, the Whig Constitution and the Hanoverian Succession were irreversible, that the balance which had been established in 1688 had been upset and could not be restored without a new revolution, and that contemporaries had not the slightest understanding of the changes which had overtaken Britain since the Glorious Revolution. He approached the politics and history of Walpolian Britain as one who fully appreciated the political significance of the massive growth in executive power which took place during the reigns of William III and Anne.[4] The Nine Years War of 1689 to 1697 and the War of the Spanish Succession from 1701 to 1714 had been vastly expensive, but they had turned Britain into an international power of the first rank, increasing her overseas and domestic trade and the wealth, military power and patronage of the Crown and its ministers. The effect of these developments on the British state had been dramatic. The Crown now had the resources to bring the troublesome Scottish kingdom under the direct control of Westminster, to neutralize unwelcome displays of political independence in Ireland and to tighten its grip on English local government, creating a cohesive *British* polity in the process. This momentous development had been the work of the Crown and a succession of Whig and Tory ministries in the 1690s and 1700s. But the Hanoverian Succession and the Jacobite Rebellion of 1715 were to have a disastrous effect on the political development of the new British state. The first had been engineered by Whigs, who seemed to be bent on hijacking the monarchy for their party. The 'Fifteen' had had the effect of tarring the Tories with Jacobitism. Government began to slip into the hands of a Whig junto led by Sir Robert Walpole, which had few scruples about deploying the vast 'influence of the Crown' to root out political opposition in the Church, Parliament and the constituencies. This was the corrupt

'Robinocracy' which was to be lampooned by the wits of Grub Street, and was thought by many to be destroying the balance of the constitution. And it was with the problem of explaining this grubby regime to his readers in mind, that Hume turned to the history of the country in which it had been born.

Walpolian Whiggery had developed in opposition to an older but still active Whiggery, as well as to the Tories. Politically and ideologically multifarious, the Whiggery of 1688 had been strikingly radical, looking back to the heroic days of the Civil War and the republican experiment which followed, and beyond that to the limited monarchies of the feudal era in which it was supposed that the power of kings had been held in check by a virtuous baronage. For some Whigs, the Glorious Revolution had been a restatement of these classic principles, reaffirming the contractual nature of government and settling the boundaries between Crown and Parliament once and for all. For others, it had been a lost opportunity which failed to take the steps which were necessary to prevent a resurgence of royal power. For these Whigs, the aristocratic junto which broke away from their radical brethren in 1696 was bent on the complete destruction of the mixed constitution by consorting with the monied interest, by advocating standing armies instead of militias, infrequent elections and, above all, the corruption on which Walpole's oligarchic government was raised.[5]

Walpolian propagandists defended these policies in the name of 'modern Whiggery'. If the influence of the Crown had increased, so had that of the Commons and it was necessary to use it to restore the balance of the constitution which had been established in 1688. In modern Britain, governments had to be strong enough to defend the Hanoverian succession and the Church from the Jacobites, to protect the empire and overseas trade, to mediate among the variety of 'jarring Interests, always opposite, often clashing' that was characteristic of modern Britain.[6] As to the charge of corruption, Lord Hervey asked in 1734, 'In what article had Liberty been infring'd? Was the Power of Parliament ever in greater Vigor? Was the Law ever more equitably administer'd? Did Men of greater Abilities, or fairer Characters, ever preside in the Courts of Justice? . . . Was there ever any Reign in which fewer Attempts were made to stretch the Bounds of the Prerogative, or fewer Abuses made of the Prerogative with its legal and proper limits?'[7] For the roots of liberty were modern, not ancient, and stemmed from the Restoration of 1660 and the Glorious Revolution, not the feudal past as old Whigs had claimed. So far as Hervey was concerned, English history before 1660 had been the story of a succession of tyrants who had inflicted their arbitrary rule on a hapless people.

> Till the Restoration there was no such thing as Liberty; [till] after the Restoration was nothing compared to the strength it gained at the Revolution, and the strength it then acquired, is so far, in my Opinion of Things, from being now impar'd, that it never flourish'd in such full Vigor as in the happy and prosperous Reign of his present Majesty.[8]

But whose interpretation of the constitution was right, the old Whigs' or the modern? Such disagreements pointed to a proposition on which Hume's understanding of politics and history depended; the authority of government simply rested on opinion. Like the Jacobites, he thought that mixed constitutions, like the British, encouraged divisions of opinion about matters of principle, and that it was all too well adjusted to encouraging faction. On the other hand, as it was the only constitution the British possessed, it was better to preserve it than to indulge in speculative and disruptive debates about constitutional theory. Teaching these uncomfortable lessons was the business of philosophers and men of letters. Every generation needs revisionists to adapt its culture to suit modern needs and Hume was to be a revisionist on a very grand scale. His analysis of British politics in the age of Walpole was to be the most terse, elegant and acute of any of that, or perhaps any other age of British history, and it is still of use today. But it was analysis with a polemical purpose, designed to make contemporaries rethink their ideas about the constitution, government and party politics, and to weigh them up against their own ideas of their interests as citizens of a state that was being transformed by war, commerce and empire. Thus it was an analysis for citizens and legislators, the 'conversable' as Hume called them; not for the learned. He wanted his readers to reflect on their political opinions and to discuss them with their friends, and he did so in the belief that the future of liberty and prosperity in modern Britain depended more on cultural than constitutional reform.

Hume chose a highly distinctive vehicle for his attempts at cultural reform which was, as he might have said, peculiar to his own age. This was a language of politeness which had developed in London in response to the political and religious zealotry of the early eighteenth century. But that story was part of another, a story about a revolution in the press which followed the inexplicable failure of the ministry to renew the Licensing Act in 1695. By this 'fit of absentmindedness' as one historian has called it, the government had relinquished its former power to control the press. The result was an astonishing expansion of the political press in London and the provinces. Some thought that this had helped to fragment and sectionalize religious and political opinion and had endangered the constitution. Others thought that the press had become a bastion of liberty, needed to preserve the independence of Parliament from an increasingly corrupt Court.[9] For Hume it was both. It was 'essential to the support of our mixed constitution' and would last 'as long as our government remains in any degree free and independent'. But as he commented, more sharply, at the end of his life, 'it must however be allowed, that the unbounded liberty of the press, though it be difficult, perhaps impossible to propose a suitable remedy for it, is one of the evils attending those mixed forms of government'.[10]

Historians have often assumed that this free press was simply a tool of party politicians, and, of course, in many respects, it was. But it is often forgotten that Grub Street developed another style of journalism that was designed to control the fragmentation of opinion by attacking the religious and political 'enthusiasm' it seemed to encourage so as to foster a public opinion that transcended party and was more 'rational', more 'moderate', more in tune with 'common sense' than that of the party propagandists. Naturally enough, many saw dark party political motives in this exercise, and sometimes they were right to do so. But, overall, the intention of this style of journalism was plain. It was to check the spread of faction and zealotry and bring about the reformation of manners needed to secure the constitution.[11]

Satire was one of the principal engines of this new culture, and no

one did more to shape it than Daniel Defoe, one of the most fascinating and attractive early-eighteenth-century denizens of Grub Street.
His long journalistic life was devoted to experimenting with the
resources of the press to manipulate opinion. He did time as a party
hack, as a ministerial agent, most notably in the matter of drumming
up support in Edinburgh for the Act of Union. He ran one of the first
great English periodicals, the *Review* (1704–13), in which he wrote
about public affairs in short, pithy essays which were discursive in
style, direct, controversial and informal in tone, and designed to
make his readers conscious of their prejudices and willing to test
them against the dictates of the 'common sense' of ordinary, sensible,
pragmatic people. His targets were opinions which caused factiousness
and what contemporaries called 'enthusiasm'; the bigotries of high-
flying churchmen, the prejudices of party zealots, the hypocrisies of
the moralists, and the bloody-mindedness of a xenophobic, ungrate-
ful and ungovernable people which he satirized in 'The True-born
Englishman'.

> William *the great Successor of* Nassau,
> Their Prayers heard, and their Oppressions saw:
> He saw and sav'd them: God and Him they prais'd;
> To this their Thanks, to that their Trophies rais'd.
> But glutted with their own Felicities,
> They soon their New Deliverer despise;
> Say all their Prayers back, their Joy disown,
> Unsing their Thanks, and pull their Trophies down:
> Their Harps of Praise are on the Willows hung;
> *For* Englishmen *are ne'er contented long*.[12]

What Defoe admired, and what he celebrated in his novel *Moll
Flanders*, was cheerful pragmatism and a willingness to get on with
the ordinary business of life, unencumbered by absurd and dangerous
prejudices, something that was just as easy for a good-natured whore
like Moll as for a city banker. In all of this Defoe appears as a satirist
on behalf of modern Whiggery, advertising the pleasures and profits
of commerce. This is what he celebrated at the end of his life in his
remarkable, still readable and still in print *A Tour through the Whole*

Island of Great Britain (1724–6). He had toured the country, not to admire its antiquities and ancient jurisdictions, but to see cities and counties which were being transformed by commerce and a country which was acquiring an elaborate system of domestic trade.

> The observations here made, as they principally regard the present state of things, so, as near as can be, they are adapted to the present taste of the times: The situation of things is given not as they have been, but as they are; the improvements in the soil, the product of the earth, the labour of the poor, the improvement in manufactures, in merchandizes, in navigation, all respects the present time, not the time past.

He continued in terms which Hume would shortly echo:

> In every country something of the people is said, as well as of the place, of their customs, speech, employments, the product of their labour, and the manner of their living, the circumstances as well as the situation of the towns, their trade and government; of the rarities of art, or nature; the rivers, of the inland and river navigation; also of the lakes and medicinal springs, not forgetting the general dependence of the whole country upon the city of London, as well for the consumption of its produce as the circulation of its trade.[13]

By the early eighteenth century, the taste for moderation and manners had established deep tap-roots in these towns and cities. This was evident from the phenomenal popular success of Joseph Addison's and Richard Steele's *Tatler* and *Spectator* essays. They were first published in 1709–13 and were endlessly reprinted and imitated in London and the provinces throughout the century, exerting a profound influence on the provincial culture of the Anglo-Saxon world at a crucial stage of its development.[14] The *Spectator* was the more reflective and admired of the two. In place of Defoe's cheerful and pungent appeals to moderation, pragmatism and profit, Addison and Steele preached the virtues of gentility and politeness as an antidote to the vagaries of opinion and the fury of faction. Their audience was ordinary citizens, women as well as men, servants, tradesmen and the young as well as persons of rank, property and position. Like Defoe, they set out to use the resources of the periodical press to preach their gospel with short, ephemeral essays on manners and morals, little moral fables and letters from their readers about the dilemmas of modern life. They wanted their readers to think of manners and morals as codes of behaviour which were useful as well as virtuous. They saw the coffee-house, the tavern and the tea-table as forums in which ordinary men and women could learn to cultivate the pleasures of friendship and refine their understanding of morality. Mr Spectator thought conversation was the best way of purging one's ideas of eccentricity and enthusiasm. What is more it brought its own rewards, by teaching that moderation in matters of opinion made one feel at home with oneself and one's companions and made one a better citizen. Politeness was to be the mother of citizenship in a genteel Spectatorial polity.

Historically, Addison and Steele were cultural entrepreneurs who set out to market classical moral codes for modern citizens. They unashamedly extolled the virtues of Cicero's *Offices*, which had presented morality as skills which could be learned in the course of ordinary life and taught men to value the virtues of the honest citizen who was temperate, fair and prudent in his dealings with others. They showed how the formal courtly rules of modern French *politesse* could be adapted to the easy, informal standards of English urban life. They agreed with their great contemporary, the 3rd Earl of Shaftesbury, that true politeness meant cultivating those naturally benevolent feelings which were all too often corrupted by imperfect taste, manners and zealotries. And, like him, they wanted to tap that innate love of perfection which fostered a love of improvement and an understanding of Christian duty.

The *Spectator* essays were not only extraordinarily wide-ranging in scope but picked up a lively popular taste for psychology, which was expressed in a vocabulary on which Hume was to draw in the hope of reaching the same huge readership as Addison. Addison taught that the opinions which shape so much of our life had their roots in the imagination, which could both enrich and corrupt the understanding. 'The unhappy Force of an Imagination unguided by the Check of Reason and Judgement' and animated by the passions could lead to 'castle-building' and to the two great errors to which religious devotion was prone: the 'madness' of enthusiasm and the 'childish' and 'idle' folly of superstition. It was society and conversation that had the power of curbing the unhappy flights of the imagination. Custom, as well as the approval of friends, had the effect of making our opinions 'habitual' and 'easie' as well as 'delightful' to us, and this in turn could explain why the modern world was filled with what Hume called 'knots and companies' of like-minded men and women.[15]

But Hume was to be a critic as well as an advocate of modern politeness. For while the polite moralists of the age were relentless and successful in advocating the improvement of manners, it was by no means clear how or why they proposed to create a new *political* culture. Defoe had no time at all for constitutional niceties, let alone the niceties of English constitutional history, and for all his robust satire he had simply appealed to the common sense of pragmatically minded, self-interested citizens. Addison's shortcomings were more interesting. For there was no apparent reason why polite coffee-house and tea-table conversation should not lead to the creation of well-organized gangs of thieves as well as coteries of good citizens. Addison himself seems to have been aware of this problem. In a group of essays in the *Spectator* he reported the activities of the Mohocks, a gang of Augustan punks who had turned much of the Strand and Covent Garden into a no-go area; they appear in his writing as an anti-club which showed how easily the virtues of politeness could be inverted by the wrong people.[16] Later on, in the much less well-known *Freeholder* essays of 1715 and 1716, which were written at the height of the Jacobite crisis, Addison went on to excoriate the 'addle-pated Sempronias' (as Swift called them) who desecrated polite tea-table conversation with displays of Jacobite and High Anglican bigotry. He complained, 'When People are accustomed to sit together with Pleasure, it is a Step towards Reconciliation: But as we manage Matters, our politest Assemblies are like boisterous Clubs, that meet over a Glass of Wine, and before they have done, throw Bottles at one anothers Heads.'[17]

Indeed, all that Addison could suggest to prevent this declension of politeness into new forms of zealotry and disorder was reading the polite authors of the ancient and modern world and cultivating the principles of natural theology. Somehow, polite citizens had to be persuaded to converse rationally about politics as well as manners, and about history as well as politics; only then would it be possible to unscramble the ideological confusions and enthusiasms which fuelled contemporary party politics; only then would contemporaries begin to understand the constitution, and the best way of preserving it. A revolution of this sort needed a critical mind capable of exploring the contradictions and confusions of contemporary culture, but it also required a degree of detachment from the hurly-burly of English politics. And while scepticism gave Hume a critical mind, Scotland provided him with a striking vantage point from which to view the progress of civilization in modern Britain.

It was not particularly difficult for Scots to distance themselves from a political world that was so deeply preoccupied with hopes and fears about the Glorious Revolution; their own revolution had been more revolutionary and less glorious than that of the English. It had brought about the re-establishment of the Presbyterian Church in its most militant form. It had given the Scots a new constitution which drastically limited the powers of the Crown and turned the Parliament and Privy Council into hotbeds of aristocratic faction. By 1700, the Scots economy was in serious trouble as well. Seven years of bad harvests had decimated the population and exposed the fragility of a backward system of agriculture. And to make matters worse William III's expensive international wars had dislocated Scotland's tenuous overseas trade and imposed huge tax burdens which a poor country with a crippled economy could ill afford to bear. By the turn of the century beggary, idleness and migration had become national scandals. Worse still, religious and political faction was being fertilized by an Anglophobia which was threatening to make Scotland ungovernable. 'God help us,' exclaimed one observer who could remember the days of the Civil War, 'we are ripening for destruction. It looks very like Forty One.'[18]

These disasters had precipitated a sustained and sophisticated debate about the condition of Scotland which began in the late 1690s and ended with the passing of the Act of Union in 1707.[19] It was a debate about which Hume seems to have been informed, and high-lighted differences between the political cultures of England and Scotland. Its theme was the problem of preserving the liberties and independence of a nation which was in danger of being destroyed by faction, poverty and the English. As one would expect, pamphleteers and politicians frequently boasted about the antiquity of the Scottish kingdom and people, their valour, their patriotism and their success in maintaining their independence for a millennium. What was more to the point was the Scottish belief that preserving liberty and inde-pendence meant major constitutional reform and encouraging the expansion of trade and commerce. Only then would they be able to keep at bay a powerful neighbour they could neither trust nor ignore. For scarcely anyone doubted that in an age of trade, commerce and empire Scotland could survive only as part of a much larger British polity. Anglophobes like the intelligent, bad-tempered and violent laird Andrew Fletcher of Saltoun looked at the problems of Scotland with classical republican eyes. He was troubled by the growth of monarchical power in modern Europe and by the massive, techno-logically advanced armies, bureaucracies and revenues that supported them. These forces were centralizing wealth, rank, talent, labour and capital in the courts of Europe, and emasculating their provinces. He dreamed of an alternative Europe composed of quasi-federated mon-archies which would be governed by sovereigns with limited powers and by regional governments dominated by rich country gentlemen like himself, who would check the growth of royal power and gener-ate economic growth in the regions. But this federal dream of a modern Scotland as part of a huge, decentralized British polity was uncomfortably reminiscent of the Dutch republic and its quarrel-some provinces, whose government had tested the political skills of that formidable politician, William of Orange, to the limit. It prompted others to take the most radical step of all, of advocating the incorporation of Scotland into a British polity ruled from Lon-don. Removing the Scottish parliament would help to destroy the cancer of faction at home, and free trade with England would stimu-late the economic growth that was needed to restore the 'independence' of an ancient nation.

By 1752, when the first volume of the *History of England* was under way, the Anglo-Scottish Union was well established. Jacobitism had been extinguished by the standing army; aristocratic and clerical faction had been contained by the patronage machine; and the middling ranks were laying the foundations of a new culture to sustain the new Union. Historically minded members of the Edinburgh *literati* had started to reflect on the significance of the changes which had taken place in the previous century. Throughout the seventeenth century, Scottish trade, learning and liberty had been put in jeopardy by the Union of the Crowns of 1603, which had placed the country in 'a strange equivocal position, little better than a conquered province'. The Glorious Revolution had given Scotland a free parliament and a free Kirk; it had even encouraged the people 'to form more extensive plans of commerce, industry and of politics', as the historian William Robertson put it. But it had needed the Union to stamp out faction, to secure property and to release that 'sudden spirit of reform' and that expansion of commerce which was characteristic of the modern age. Like Hume, the Scots realized that, until property was secure and government was regular, neither commerce nor civilization was possible. That prospect had been opened up by the Union. As the first *Edinburgh Review* of 1755–6 put it, 'If countries have had their ages with respect to improvement, North Britain may be considered as in a state of early youth guided and supported by the more mature strength of her kindred country.'[20]

Here was an image of Scotland – or rather North Britain – as part of a new British polity, freed from faction and poverty, exposed to the civilizing powers of commerce, having acquired a culture capable of exploiting it. This was the world to which Hume belonged and whose commitment to commerce he celebrated in essays of unrivalled cogency and sophistication which were written in 1752 as he set to work on the *History*. To those who argued that commerce fostered luxury and made men self-regarding, covetous and effeminate, Hume replied that its tendency was to encourage industry and knowledge:

> In times when industry and the arts flourish, men are kept in perpetual occupation, and enjoy, as their reward, the occupation itself, as well as those pleasures which are the fruit of their labour. The mind acquires

new vigour; enlarges its powers and faculties; and, by an assiduity in honest industry, both satisfies its natural appetites, and prevents the growth of unnatural ones, which commonly spring up, when nourished by ease and idleness. Banish those arts from society, you deprive men both of action and of pleasure; and, leaving nothing but indolence in their place, you even destroy the relish of indolence, which never is agreeable, but when it succeeds to labour, and recruits the spirits, exhausted by too much application and fatigue.

So, far from corrupting, commerce civilized, stimulating refinements in the arts and sciences, and increasing sociability and humanity in the process.

The more these refined arts advance, the more sociable men become: nor is it is possible, that, when enriched with science, and possessed of a fund of conversation, they should be contented to remain in solitude, or live with their fellow-citizens in that distant manner, which is peculiar to ignorant and barbarous nations. They flock into cities; love to receive and communicate knowledge; to show their wit or their breeding; their taste in conversation or living, in clothes or furniture. Curiosity allures the wise; vanity the foolish; and pleasure both. Particular clubs and societies are everywhere formed: both sexes meet in an easy and sociable manner; and the tempers of men, as well as their behaviour, refine apace. So that, beside the improvements which they receive from knowledge and the liberal arts, it is impossible but they must feel an increase of humanity, from the very habit of conversing together, and contributing to each other's pleasure and entertainment. Thus *industry, knowledge,* and *humanity* are linked together, by an indissoluble chain, and are found, from experience as well as reason, to be peculiar to the more polished, and, what are commonly denominated, the more luxurious ages. [21]

Thus, while commerce could never progress until property was secure, it had the natural tendency to beget social order and to stamp out the factiousness and warfare that was the bane of civilization. 'Laws, order, police, discipline; these can never be carried to any degree of perfection, before human reason has refined itself by exercise, and by an application to the more vulgar arts, at least of commerce and manufacture.' This must make men less intractable. 'Factions are then less inveterate, revolutions less tragical, authority less severe, and seditions less frequent. Even foreign wars abate of their cruelty; and after the field of battle, where honour and interest steel men against compassion, as well as fear, the combattants divest themselves of the brute and resume the man.'[22]

Here was the Scottish spokesman for a culture which held that commerce had the power to civilize, that its roots lay in the modern world and that it required new political institutions and a new culture to support it. Like any Scot of his class, Hume had seen how patronage could be used to contain the faction that had threatened to destroy his country's independence; he had seen how patriots, living in a newly stable world, could rebuild its economy and culture. This was the context in which he turned to the task of reconstructing the political culture of the Walpolian world; here that he learned how the polite languages of Grub Street could be developed to serve very much more ambitious purposes. Addison had shown how human beings become sociable; Hume wanted to show that fresh thinking about the constitution could help them become civilized. It would mean teaching Addison's readers to think about politics as well as manners; and about history as well as politics. It meant showing Defoe's readers and those who read ministerial propaganda *why* the roots of civilization were modern and *why* civilization had been impossible in the early ages of English history. Only then would it be possible to reinforce their appeals to common sense and personal interest with history and philosophy. Only then would it be possible to unscramble the ideological confusions and enthusiasms which had fuelled faction. Only then would the English have the benefit of a truly Scottish understanding of the foundations of the modern constitution and the effects of commerce on its development.

3

Scepticism, Science and the Natural History of Man

Hume was to write about the politics and history of Britain as a sceptic who had constructed a science of man on experimental principles. But it is impossible to understand the subtle interplay of scepticism, science and history in Hume's thought unless one remembers that his account of the principles of human nature was not only secular but planned and executed as a devastating attack on Christianity. For Christians had always claimed – and perhaps still do – that pagans or infidels who did not share their Christian understanding could not possibly provide a complete account of the principles of human nature. It was a claim which carried an assumption that Hume found intolerable; that Christians possessed a monopoly of wisdom, virtue and patriotism. It was not surprising that Boswell thought him serious in asserting 'flatly that the morality of every religion was bad'; not for nothing that he once remarked 'the Church is my particular Aversion'.[1]

In the *Treatise of Human Nature*, Hume set out to show that a pagan who drew on the resources of ancient scepticism and modern experimental science could develop an account of the principles of human nature which was *better* than that of the Christians in the sense that it was more closely textured, more coherent and thus more plausible than theirs. It also allowed him to show that the natural tendency of Christian theology and morality was to distort men's understanding of truth and duty, destabilize human society and pervert the course of human happiness. When he turned to the history of England, he was to emphasize the malign effects of priestcraft and religious zealotry on English history and was to argue that the roots

of the English constitution and the rage of party lay in religious superstition and enthusiasm. What is remarkable, biographically speaking,
is that this campaign against the pretensions of Christianity had
begun as early as 1729, when Hume was only eighteen. Its first fruits
were to be seen ten years later, with the publication of the *Treatise of
Human Nature.*

We shall probably never know exactly when, how and why Hume
lost his belief in Christianity and became interested in scepticism and
science; his early life is very poorly documented. As the devoted son
of a kindly and pious strict Presbyterian mother, it is not surprising
that he remembered being religious as a child. In fact, Boswell's
account of his death-bed conversation with Hume gives fascinating
and plausible glimpses of what seems to have been an orthodox religious upbringing and what must have been his first and most
fundamental intellectual experience – his curiosity about the *authority* on which the moral teaching of the Church rested.

> I know not [Boswell said] how I contrived to get the subject of immor-
> tality introduced. He said he had never entertained any belief in
> religion since he began to read Locke and Clarke. I asked if he was not
> religious when he was young. He said he was, and used to read *The
> Whole Duty of Man*; that he made an abstract from the catalogue of
> vices at the end of it, and examined himself by this, leaving out murder
> and theft and such vices as he had no chance of committing, having no
> inclination to commit them. This, he said, was strange work; for
> instance, to try if, notwithstanding his excelling his schoolfellows, he
> had no pride or vanity.'[2]

By the mid-1720s, a few years before the 'new scene of thought'
opened up to him, Hume had evidently decided that theologians
were unable to give any adequate reasons for believing in the existence of God or for crediting the Deity with the moral authority which
Christians thought he possessed. He had probably also acquired a
nodding acquaintance with scepticism and modern science and had
realized that both systems of thought had been permeated by Christian theology. In the *Treatise* Hume was to strip off these theological
accretions and create an analytical framework for a new sceptical

science of man. It may sound like a contradiction in terms to describe Hume's science of man as 'sceptical'; after all, we are accustomed to think of Bacon, Boyle and Newton and their followers as scientists who had generated real knowledge about the world from cautious experimentation and had given man power over nature in consequence. But every popular philosopher and theologian of Hume's age knew that radical sceptics claimed to be able to show that knowledge and that so-called truths about morality, politics, religion and science were only opinions. It was thus impossible to know the world, let alone change it. The best one could do was to learn the virtue of indifference and live as quietly and undogmatically as possible according to the customs and traditions of the age.

The intellectual core of radical or Pyrrhonian scepticism was contained in a highly complicated system of logic which had been devised in the fourth century BC by the Greek philosopher Pyrrho and developed by his disciple Sextus Empiricus, whose *Hypotyposes* were rediscovered and republished in 1562. Sextus' logic showed that it was impossible to formulate any general statement about the world which could be verified by means of reason or the senses and regarded as more likely to be true than any other. No doubt this conclusion was useful in dealing with dogmatists and zealots. But its larger implications were much more troubling. Reducing all knowledge to opinion meant reducing all certainties to probabilities and undermining the claims of theology and experimental science to be exact disciplines, capable of generating real knowledge about the world. At the same time it had the most alarming implications for morality by devaluing the heroic and saintly values for which stoic and Christian moralists stood. 'Oh miserable Pyrrho, who has made all into opinion and indifference' was the constant complaint of moralists from the sixteenth to the eighteenth centuries.[3]

It did not take long for Protestant and Catholic theologians to respond to the challenge of scepticism by turning it to Christian advantage. As Montaigne showed in his extraordinary *Apologie de Raimond Sebond* (1580), Pyrrhonian analysis could yield devotional benefits. Rigorous thought experiments had demonstrated the frailty of reason and the senses and their inability to provide him with knowledge about the world. It was a humbling discovery which had stripped him of his intellectual pride, and prepared him to wait for God to release the faith he needed to understand a world which was beyond the range of intellectual comprehension. As Cleanthes is made to say in the *Dialogues Concerning Natural Religion*, 'You think that if certainty or evidence be expelled from every other subject of enquiry, it will all retire to these theological doctrines, and there acquire a superior force and authority.'4 By the late seventeenth century, Pyrrhonian scepticism had acquired a new and formidable Christian face, in the person of the French Oratorian priest Nicolas de Malebranche, whose *Recherche sur la Verité* (1672) was well known in Hume's Britain in polite as well as in philosophical circles; Addison even thought that every well-educated lady ought to have a copy of this singularly taxing work in her cabinet.5

This alone would have made Malebranche's philosophy worth Hume's attention, but Hume had other reasons for studying this Christian philosopher. Like so many others, he had learned his Christianity as a child from *The Whole Duty of Man*, that austere primer which was designed to teach the young about sin, the nature of fallen man and the duties he owed to the Deity, by whose grace alone he could be redeemed. Malebranche provided an equally fashionable but infinitely more sophisticated account of the same strict view of Christianity which was all the more interesting to Hume because it claimed to have scotched the sceptical serpent and to have demonstrated that reason did indeed have the power to regulate our conduct. For Malebranche had provided the classic modern description of fallen Christian man. He was a creature who was capable of reason but was generally driven by the passions; able to exercise free will but too easily governed by necessity; caught between the eternal world of God and the time-bound world of circumstance and history. As he put it in the first sentence of his long book, 'The Mind of Man is by its Nature situated, as it were, between its Creator and Corporeal Creatures, for according to St Augustine, there is nothing above it but God alone, and nothing but Bodies below it.'6 In our earthly, fallen state, it was inevitable that our minds would be deluded by the passions, the senses and the imagination and that we would squander

our chances of eternal happiness in the pursuit of the ephemeral sat-
isfactions of earthly pleasure. The task of the Christian philosopher
was to provide the anxious Christian with irrefutable evidence that he
had a mind which was distinct from his body and the ability to understand God's purposes and the duties we owed him. Like his great
master Descartes, Malebranche used sceptical reasoning to investigate
the contents of the mind and the endless mutable fantasies with which
it seemed to be furnished. His purpose was to enquire whether we
possessed any clear, distinct and stable ideas which were impervious
to the corruptions of the imagination, and whose truth could not be
doubted. What he discovered was a metaphysical world of ideas
about ideas, which did indeed satisfy these conditions. For however
disordered and corrupt the world of the imagination might seem to
be, we cannot doubt that we have minds and live in a causally determined world. Indeed, without such beliefs, life would be impossible.
Malebranche was able to conclude that reason has the power to pen-
etrate the earthly, time-bound world of illusion, to discover the fixed
eternal truths which lie beyond it, and to recognize the path to eternal
happiness in a divinely created world. Thus, by '[looking] within
themselves' anyone could discover the power of reason to give them
access to the mind of God, 'who is our only Master, and who can
teach us Truth, by the Manifestation of his Substance.'[7]

We simply do not know when or how Hume made contact with
scepticism ancient and modern, pagan and Christian. It is possible
that he first encountered it in a devotional context from a Christian
who wanted to help a sophisticated boy rebuild his shaky faith; as one
would expect, the value of sceptical reasoning was well known in
strict Presbyterian circles in Scotland.[8] As an Edinburgh student in the
1720s, he would have had relatively easy access to crucial texts like
Cicero's *Academics*, Bayle's *Dictionary*, Montaigne's *Essays* and Malebranche's *Recherche*. Hume presumably made his first serious contacts
with scepticism in the later 1720s when he was still a student, slipping
out of his belief in Christianity and encountering modern science; as
we shall see, experimental science was to play a crucial role in shaping
his science of man. If the religious hypothesis was to be scotched, he
had to show that there were better ways of explaining how we come

to think of the world as orderly and coherent than those of the Christians; and that demonstration had to be proof against the sceptics. Hume thought that such an explanation could come only from a mechanical philosophy which explained the principles of metaphysical order in the same way as the great natural philosophers of the previous century had explained it in the physical world. Such thinking was common enough in his student days. Natural philosophers like Boyle and Newton had been able to present the physical world as a material world in which bodies acted and reacted systematically upon each other. Medical scientists, like Archibald Pitcairne and Alexander Monro, had described the workings of the 'animal economy' in similar terms and had shown that the different functions of the body were controlled by the nervous system and the fluids and ethers which activated it. Political scientists like Andrew Fletcher of Saltoun and John Trenchard had attempted to describe politics in terms of the behaviour of passionate and self-regarding human beings whose behaviour could be shaped and turned to the public advantage by well-adjusted constitutions. Such modes of mechanical thinking were to be found in the university and in the salons of Edinburgh in the 1720s and 1730s; in the lectures of professors like Colin MacLaurin, Newton's favourite pupil; in discussions of Boyle which were held in the Natural Philosophy class, of which Hume seems to have been a member; and in the fashionable political writings of Trenchard and Lord Bolingbroke, whose *Cato's Letters* and *Craftsman* were widely available.

But, once again, modern science, like modern scepticism, had become deeply penetrated by theology. Boyle, Newton and the doctors of Edinburgh and Glasgow all found it impossible to settle for a purely mechanical description of the natural world as a self-sustaining, homeostatic order whose function was simply to regulate itself; after all, as strict Christians pointed out, that simply led to deism or materialism and unsettled Christian belief in man as a being who was capable of perfecting himself and the world in which he lived. As Colin MacLaurin put it,

> The philosopher who overlooks [the traces of an all-governing deity], contenting himself with the appearances of the material universe only,

and the mechanical laws of motion, neglects what is most excellent; and prefers what is imperfect to what is supremely perfect, finitude to infinity, what is narrow and weak to what is unlimited and almighty, and what is perishing to what endures for ever.[9]

No Western philosopher was more troubled by the pressures of scepticism and science on Christian thinking than Francis Hutcheson, the Scots-Irish professor of moral philosophy at Glasgow from 1729 to 1746, whom Hume always regarded as one of the founders of modern philosophy. Hutcheson did not believe that the principles of human nature could be described in terms of the opposition of reason and the passions, as orthodox Christians like Malebranche thought. If that were true, either morality was an intellectual skill which could be mastered only by Christians who had a rational insight into the mind of the Creator, or it was simply a cynical cloak to self-interest. Neither view took account of the fact that human beings seem to warm to those who behave virtuously and have a natural desire to act virtuously. What is more, most of our moral behaviour seems to be regular and patterned and to be derived from our experience of common life. Hutcheson's elaborate analysis of the principles which regulate our moral behaviour led him to conclude that it was regulated by a faculty which he called the moral sense. It was the source of our natural curiosity in the moral behaviour of others; it ensured that we would always think of our own interests in relation to theirs; it enabled us to enjoy the spectacle of moral order rather as we enjoy order in architecture or painting; it seemed to increase our understanding of order and lead us to revere the deity who had created it. It was, thus, 'universal calm Benevolence', not reason, that had the power 'to limit and counteract not only the Selfish Passions, but even the particular kind affections', Hutcheson concluded.

> Our moral Sense shews this to be the highest Perfection of our Nature; what we may see to [be] the End or Design of such a Structure, and consequently what is requir'd of us by the Author of our Nature: and therefore if anyone like these Descriptions better, he may call Virtue, with many of the Antients, 'Vita secundum naturam; or

acting according to what we may see from the Constitution of our Nature, we were intended for by our Creator'.[10]

It was a sensational discovery. Here, it seemed, was a new sense, hitherto unknown to philosophy, which was proof against the sceptics and provided new proofs for the existence of a far less austere deity than that of the orthodox Christians; a deity who presided over a naturally sociable world and offered mankind the chance of happiness in this world as well as the next. It was no wonder that Hutcheson became one of the most admired moral philosophers of his time, and it was scarcely surprising that Hume should have had him as well as Malebranche in mind when he divested modern philosophy of its theological trappings and located the study of human behaviour in the world of common life and history.

Hume began his *Treatise of Human Nature* by complaining about the constant wranglings of philosophers over the principles of human nature, and by announcing that he would offer a new account which was based on the observation of human behaviour and not on theological premises.

> And tho' we must endeavour to render all our principles as universal as possible, by tracing up our experiments to the utmost, and explaining all effects from the simplest and fewest causes, 'tis still certain we cannot go beyond experience; and any hypothesis, that pretends to discover the ultimate original qualities of human nature, ought at first to be rejected as presumptuous and chimerical.

Thus 'We must . . . glean up our experiments in this science from a cautious observation of human life, and take them as they appear in the common course of the world, by men's behaviour in company, in affairs and in their pleasures.'[11]

The first and crucial stage of the enquiry was to discover whether the distinction between mind and body on which Malebranche's philosophy rested could be verified experimentally. More particularly, he wanted to discover whether reason really did have the power to regulate the passions as Malebranche had claimed. This distinction seemed to lie at the heart of all Christian theology; if it stood the test of experiment, there would be a secure foundation for Christian theology. If not, Christianity would be exposed as a myth. For notwithstanding Hutcheson's experiments on the moral sense, with which Hume would deal later, he concluded: 'If we distrust human reason, we have now no other principle to lead us into religion.'[12]

And myth is what Hume proved religion to be. No one could have analysed the Malebranchean portrait of Christian man with more seriousness than he did. He once told a close Christian friend, Sir Gilbert Elliot of Minto, that in working out his philosophy, he had 'begun with an anxious Search after Arguments, to confirm the common Opinion: Doubts stole in, dissipated, return'd, were again dissipated, return'd again; and it was a perpetual Struggle of a restless Imagination against Inclination, perhaps against Reason'.[13] He stated the arguments he wanted to examine in the strongest possible form; he conducted Pyrrhonian thought-experiments of the utmost rigour on himself, shutting himself away from society and even, perhaps, experimenting with his diet and losing weight in the process, in order to study the effect of social and bodily appetites on the mind. All of this was recorded in a notebook, later destroyed, in which he traced 'page after page, the gradual Progress of my thoughts on that head'.[14] The results of his analysis were extraordinary. Malebranche had shown that, although the mind appeared to be a prisoner of the imagination and its constantly shifting desires and fantasies, reason was capable of liberating it from its bondage by showing that we inhabit an orderly metaphysical world in which we could find a new understanding of ourselves and our duties to our Creator. But Hume's Pyrrhonian scepticism showed, quite conclusively, that the metaphysical world Malebranche thought he had discovered was as disordered as the world of the imagination. What is more, he discovered that the harder he pressed his reason to discover the structure of these metaphysical ideas, the more they fragmented in a never-ending process of regression:

> Let our first belief be never so strong, it must infallibly perish by passing thro' so many new examinations, of which each diminishes somewhat of its force and vigour. When I reflect on the natural fallibility of my judgement, I have less confidence in my opinions, than when I only

consider the objects concerning which I reason; and when I proceed still farther, to turn the scrutiny against every successive estimation I make of my faculties, all the rules of logic require a continual diminution, and at last a total extinction of belief and evidence.[15]

In the process 'all knowledge degenerates into probability; and this probability is greater or less, according to our experience of the veracity or deceitfulness of our understanding, and according to the simplicity or intricacy of the question'.[16] Reason was incapable of regulating the mind; indeed, a mind unregulated by reason could hardly be said to be a mind at all. 'What we call a mind', Hume wrote, 'is nothing but a heap or collection of different perceptions, united together by certain relations, and supposed, tho' falsely, to be endowed with a perfect simplicity and identity.'[17] And, if we had no minds, could we be said to have identities; could we be said to exist at all? For like the mind, a man is 'nothing but a bundle or collection of different perceptions, which succeed each other with an inconceivable rapidity, and are in a perpetual flux and movement'.[18] It was from the imagination that we derived all our understanding of metaphysics, morals, politics, religion, science and even of our own identities. It was the imagination which was 'the ultimate judge of all systems of philosophy'.[19] It was for this reason that Hume concluded that we had been consigned to a metaphysical wilderness, to the 'Universe of the Imagination'.[20]

These thought-experiments produced an unexpected conclusion of great interest. However hard he had tried to force his reason to tread the self-destructive path of metaphysical speculation, Hume was completely unable to carry his analysis to its logical conclusion; after all, deconstructing the mind had meant deconstructing the self. He noticed that, in the last resort, nature, in the form of the passions, always stepped in to rescue him from annihilation by forcing him to believe in some of the ideas he was deconstructing rather than others and thus returning him to the world of common life.

> The *intense* view of these manifold contradictions and imperfections in human reason has so wrought upon me, and heated my brain, that I am ready to reject all belief and reasoning, and can look upon no opinion

even as more probable or likely than another. Where am I, or what? From what causes do I derive my existence, and to what condition shall I return? Whose favour shall I court, and whose anger must I dread? What beings surround me? and on whom have I any influence, or who have any influence on me? I am confounded with all these questions, and begin to fancy myself in the most deplorable condition imaginable, inviron'd with the deepest darkness, and utterly depriv'd of the use of every member and faculty.

Most fortunately it happens, that since reason is incapable of dispelling these clouds, nature herself suffices to that purpose, and cures me of this philosophical melancholy and delirium, either by relaxing this bent of mind, or by some avocation, and lively impression of my senses, which obliterate all these chimeras. I dine, I play a game of back-gammon, I converse, and am merry with my friends; and when after three or four hours' amusement, I wou'd return to these speculations, they appear so cold, and strain'd, and ridiculous, that I cannot find in my heart to enter into them again.[21]

Here was evidence that the purpose of the passions was to preserve rather than corrupt, to rescue us from reason which seemed bent on our destruction and to return us to the sociable world in which philosophers, like everyone else, had been raised before embarking on their quixotic metaphysical escapades. So far as Hume was concerned, it was a forcible reminder that he had embarked on his adventures as a man whose understanding of the world had already been determined by the customs, conventions and education of common life, and the metaphysical crisis he had experienced had simply served to remind him that the world into which he had been born was one from which it would be impossible to escape. It was the only world in which philosophers, like the men in the street, could hope to find security and happiness. Hume had shown that Christian claims that it was possible to discern the ultimate nature of reality and virtue through the use of reason was not only spurious but dangerous. It was the first stage in what was to become a life-long running attack on Christianity and it would have the most profound consequences for his understanding of the philosophical uses of history.

If Hume's scepticism is viewed through orthodox Christian eyes, he could be said to have collapsed mind into body, and to have consigned mortals to a purposeless life directed by the ever-changing whims and fancies of the imagination. In fact, he had done something far more interesting. He had shown that nature requires us to believe in some ideas rather than others and that the ideas we believe in are those which we find necessary for ordinary life. He had also been able to show that although the metaphysical ideas which make all forms of thought possible – our beliefs in the existence of an external world, in the necessary relationship of cause and effect, in the substantiality of objects, for example – had their origins in the imagination and the experience of common life, it was wrong to think of them as transient whims or fancies for the simple reason that they *feel* fixed, settled, inescapable and 'true' and they feel like this because they are necessary to our survival and happiness. They were the foundation stones on which our 'understanding' of the world depended. For in Hume's philosophy, while we could never reach what the theologians thought of as 'knowledge' of the world, we could aspire to an 'understanding' which was derived from the experience of this world rather than the next.

This suggestion was of immense importance to Hume in shaping his understanding of history. He had shown that we owe our understanding of the world to a process of cognitive education which takes place in the time-bound, historically determined societies in which we find ourselves. But these societies, these scenes of life, as contemporaries sometimes described them, had their own histories which were of fundamental importance in shaping the minds and characters of the individuals who inhabited them. History, as Hume was coming to understand it, was to be thought of in terms of the life-span of individuals, societies and civilizations and in the interaction between them. It was as important for the Humean to understand the multilayered nature of historical time as it was to the Christian to understand the nature of eternity. Hume's loathing of Christianity had presented him with history in its deepest sense as the replacement for theology and the key to weaning modern citizens from a dangerously mythic world.

But Hume had much more work to do before the full force of his first insights into the principles of human nature could be presented as a fully developed theory of human nature. In the first place he had to explore the educational process which allows us to form ideas and sentiments about the world, and he had to undertake the all-important task of considering its effects on the working of the passions. His discussion had already hinted at the crucial role of language and conversation in shaping our ideas and sentiments although interestingly this was not a subject he chose to explore. But this line of argument suggested that there was some fundamental principle at work which made social intercourse possible and explained the workings of the conventions on which the understanding depended. This was the principle of sympathy, a term well known to contemporary philosophy and to the readers of the polite press but one which Hume now proceeded to give powerful philosophical leverage.

> No quality of human nature is more remarkable, both in itself and in its consequences, than that propensity we have to sympathize with others, and to receive by communication their inclinations and sentiments, however different from, or even contrary to our own. This is not only conspicuous in children, who implicitly embrace every opinion propos'd to them: but also in men of the greatest judgement and understanding, who find it very difficult to follow their own reason or inclination, in opposition to that of their friends and daily companions. To this principle we ought to ascribe the great uniformity we may observe in the humours and turn of thinking of those of the same nations.[22]

For it was sympathy that made it possible for human beings to enter into the beliefs and sentiments of others and to turn them to their own uses, and it was this that allowed whole societies to develop the common cultures on which their national characteristics depended. Hume was now in a position to consider the effect of the understanding on the passions, a task he undertook in Book 2 of the *Treatise*, 'Of the Passions'. It went almost without saying that the primary function of the passions was to serve what we imagined to be our interests at any particular moment. But Hume's analysis had shown that ideas of 'interest' and 'self' were themselves the fruits of the forms of understanding we derived from our experience of common life and it was this that made it possible for him to develop a remarkable account of the working of the passions. This emphasized the extent to which passions were shaped by social conventions and customs. Thus my sense of pride in my family, fortune and possessions presupposes my living in a society in which such things are regarded as a legitimate expression of pride. Thus my capacity for love and hatred presupposes a similar world of conventions which shape my emotions and prescribe the language of response which will shape my subsequent conduct. Indeed, Hume remarked, so deeply are our passions penetrated by convention, that 'we can form no wish, which has not a reference to society'.[23]

By now Hume was ready to consider how we acquire those beliefs in the necessity of rules of justice, morality and political obligation for the maintenance of society, and how we acquire the corresponding belief that it is our duty to obey them.

Hume had already disposed of the view that reason alone has the power to convince us of the importance of subscribing to such ideas if we are to survive and prosper in civil society. Now he was ready to dispose of Hutcheson's view that this power was invested in a moral sense which would always incline us to regard and treat others benevolently. Hume came to the opposite conclusion, arguing that by themselves, benevolent feelings were profoundly anti-social. For human beings are generally influenced by considerations of interest and 'even when they extend their concern beyond themselves, 'tis not to any great distance: nor is it usual for them, in common life, to look farther than their nearest friends and acquaintances'.[24] To be sure, as gregarious beings, their 'natural uncultivated ideas of morality' would encourage them to do what they could for their families and friends, and this generally meant making them gifts. But gift-giving of this sort could usually only be done at the expense of others, with potentially disastrous consequences for social order. As Hume wrote, 'this avidity alone of acquiring goods or possessions for ourselves and our friends is insatiable, perpetual, universal and directly destructive of society'.[25] Society was only possible when every citizen had learned by force, persuasion, habit or conviction to restrain a fundamental instinct in the expectation that they would gain more from restraining than indulging it. Learning to restrain our acquisitive passions was the hard lesson every individual had to learn if he was to survive and prosper in society. Indeed, it was the rock on which an individual's understanding of justice and his or her capacity for sociability depended.

Hume went out of his way to show how difficult it could be for men and women to acquire a sense of justice, even if they had grown up in a civilized society. No one in any state of society could be expected to curb his natural acquisitiveness until he was reasonably sure that others would do the same. As Hume put it, ''tis only on the expectation of this, that our moderation and abstinence are founded'.[26] The roots of our ideas of justice were, like any other, formed in 'company and conversation' and embedded in the conventions and language on which social discourse depends, 'thus, two men pull the oars of a boat by common interest, without any promise or contract: thus gold and silver are made the measure of exchange: thus speech and words and language are fixed by human convention and agreement.'[27]

But while such conventions were necessary for the maintenance of society, in real life there would always be individuals who would be beguiled by the imagination into believing that their interests would be better served by a policy of grab and run than by restraint. Indeed, so far as Hume was concerned, the only reason we can have for establishing and obeying political authority was that it was needed to preserve our property. Nor could any society be said to be truly stable until its rulers were obeyed out of habit. Nothing, said Hume, 'is more conformable, both to prudence and morals than to submit quietly to the government, which we find establish'd in the country where we happen to live, without enquiring too curiously into its origin and first establishment'.[28] In other words, political authority was the mother of justice and its regular exercise was the rock on which civilization was founded. And the sense of political obligation which regular government engendered would foster a respect for property, encourage tolerance, virtue and humanity, and release the inquisitiveness and inventiveness on which the progress of civilization depended. Only then would citizens be in a position to understand the *utility* of government to common life.

In the last resort, then, it was as important to understand the political constitution of a country as it was to understand the constitution of the mind if one was to understand how a citizen was to live sociably and virtuously. Hume knew very well that the constitution of savage societies which were not based on systems of private property would be very different from that of property-based societies. And he accepted the commonplace distinction that pastoral societies based on herding, and feudal societies based on agriculture, would develop different sorts of constitution to the modern, increasingly commercialized societies of his own day. Indeed his *History of England* would explore the effects of different types of constitution on the development of English civilization. But the question of the best type of constitution in any form of civilization remained. His analysis pointed to the stark conclusion that the best constitutions were those which were able to sustain a form of government which was stable, secure and best able to absorb the shock of a mediocre or incompetent ruler. Constitutions which were simple and in which power was undivided and undisputed were, by definition, better able to secure the habitual obedience of subjects than those in which the powers of rulers were limited or divided, particularly when, as was the case in Britain, those dividing lines were uncertain and contentious. In the same way, constitutions which favoured hereditary succession tended to be better able to ensure stable government than those which provided for elective succession. In such cases citizens would have less reason to question the legitimacy of rulers and engage in abstract ideological speculations about the principles of political authority which could be manipulated by unscrupulous priests and politicians and deflect their attention from the public interest. And in stable societies of this sort it would be easier for subjects to acquire a sense of liberty.

Hume's discussion of politics presupposed the view of political prudence he expected of subjects and their rulers. A prudent subject was a citizen who was prepared to take the constitution as he found it and who was willing to accept that while its operations might be improved and regularized, its fundamental principles could not be altered without a revolution which would undermine society itself. A prudent ruler was one who attempted to maintain the authority of government and was interested in regularizing its operations. In the hands of a Walpole, that might involve the use of corruption. In the hands of Edward I, the utmost severity. In the hands of Elizabeth, deceit, imperiousness and bluff. For the techniques of prudent government depended on the peculiarities of the constitution and on the culture of the age in which rulers found themselves. Rulers who were unable to maintain their authority would quickly discover that faction would thrive, the security of property would be weakened and the progress of civilization would be endangered. This was why Hume was to launch some of his bitterest attacks on rulers who tried to interfere with their subjects' peaceful enjoyment of their property or who encouraged the ultimate folly of attempting a general redistribution of property in the name of creating an imaginary vision of a more perfect society.

> Historians, and even common sense, may inform us, that, however specious these ideas of *perfect* equality may seem, they are really at bottom, *impracticable*; and were they not so, would be extremely *pernicious* to human society. Render possessions ever so equal, men's different degrees of art, care, and industry will immediately break that equality. Or if you check these virtues, you reduce society to the most extreme indigence; and instead of preventing want and beggary in a few, render it unavoidable to the whole community. The most rigorous inquisition too is requisite to watch every inequality on its first appearance; and the most severe jurisdiction, to punish and redress it.[29]

By now, Hume had reached the limits of the science of man he had discussed in the *Treatise*. He had examined the processes by which human beings become sociable and the education that was required to turn them into citizens. In doing so he had urged his readers to reflect on their own experience of common life, and the history of the societies to which they belonged if they wanted to understand themselves and the duties they owed to their fellow citizens and their sovereign. It was now time to move from the general to the particular, from the natural history of the species to the civil histories of particular countries with particular constitutional arrangements. For Hume, this meant turning to the history of his own country, to its mixed and unsettled constitution, to a political life that was plagued by faction and infected by ideology and religion, and all of this at a time when the social and economic fabric of the country was being transformed by commerce. Above all, it meant teaching Britons the meaning of political prudence.

4

A Philosopher's Agenda for a History of England

If one takes Hume's ambitions to apply philosophy to public life seriously, then the early 1740s form a watershed in his career. This was when he turned from natural to civil history and to the politics of contemporary Britain. By the time the second and final volume of the *Treatise* appeared in 1740, this new enterprise was already under way. Hume had already used British examples to illustrate his political theory and he appears to have been working on the political and moral essays he was to publish in 1741 at the same time. However, it was clear that, if these essays were to be read, they would have to be popular, and that meant exploiting the resources of the popular press. At first, he thought of establishing a new periodical paper with the help of his friend Henry Home, the future judge and *littérateur* Lord Kames, but the plan fell through.[1] Instead, the short volume of *Essays Moral and Political* was published in 1741 and was followed up by two more in 1742 and 1747. These provided an analysis of British politics at the end of the Walpolian era for a popular audience. They also provided an agenda for a history of civilization in England.

Hume wanted to show how learning and letters could be used to reform the political culture of modern Britain. In the *Treatise* he had shown that a pagan could provide a better account of the principles of human nature than a strict or moderate Christian. In the *Essays*, he did exactly the same thing, taking as his targets Addison's popular *Spectator* essays and the influential political essays Bolingbroke had written for the *Craftsman*, the leading opposition journal. Mr Spectator's readers were to be shown that politics was important to polite discourse. Bolingbroke's were to be shown the dangers of attempting to use politeness for party political purposes. 'Public Spirit . . . shou'd engage us to love the Public, and to bear an equal affection to all our Country-Men; not to hate one Half of them under Pretext of loving the Whole', Hume wrote.[2] For his target was 'party rage' and his principal purpose was to show how party politics could be discussed impartially and with moderation.

Hume began by recasting his metaphysics in the language of Addisonian politeness. His philosophy had demonstrated the importance of conversation and language in shaping and socializing human behaviour, and these concerns were of central importance to polite moralists. Hume wanted to show that citizens could improve their political judgement by lacing polite conversation with something more nutritious than the tittle-tattle of the tavern and the tea-table which Addison's 'agreeable trifflings' had encouraged.[3] 'Must our whole discourse be a continual series of gossiping stories and idle remarks?' Hume complained. 'Must the mind never rise higher, but be perpetually

> Stunn'd and worn out with endless chat,
> Of Will did this and Nan did that.'

Cultivating 'the liberal arts and sciences' was the best way of saving the 'conversible' members of society from this fate,

> and to that end, I know nothing more advantageous than such Essays as those with which I endeavour to entertain the public. In this view, I cannot but consider myself as a kind of resident or ambassador from the dominions of learning to those of conversation, and shall think it my constant duty to promote a good correspondence betwixt these two states, which have so great a dependence on each other.[4]

Reading and discussing the arts and sciences would help to improve the judgement. It would make a person 'indifferent to the company and conversation of the greater part of men' and more selective in his choice of friends.

> And his affections being thus confined within a narrower circle, no wonder he carries them further than if they were more general and

undistinguished. The gaity and frolic of a bottle companion improves with him into a solid friendship; and the ardour of a youthful appetite becomes an elegant passion.[5]

With these deceptively simple flourishes, Hume was able to identify his future audience. It was to be 'the elegant part of mankind', intelligent and thoughtful men and women – Hume always insisted that his writing was addressed to both sexes – who, like him, belonged to 'the middling ranks' of society. They were too rich to be servile to the great, too poor to tyrannize the humble. Their values were urban rather than rustic; they were naturally gregarious, and independent-minded. They were 'the most numerous rank of men that can be supposed susceptible of philosophy' to whom therefore all discourses of morality ought to be addressed.[6] They had won their independence of the nobility with the decline of feudal tenures; they had profited from the growth of commerce. On the other hand, their political and moral culture had been shaped by the religious turmoil unleashed by the Reformation and by the political and religious conflicts of the seventeenth century. As Hume was to show in the *History of England*, their fortunes and those of the Matchless Constitution were inextricably intertwined, and until they understood the history and culture of their own class and country and learned to adapt it to modern circumstances, the future of civilization in Britain would remain uncertain.

Hume's essays made heavy demands on his readers, and only a Scot wedded to the politics of politeness would have dared to make them. Indeed, it is much easier to imagine his essays fertilizing conversation in Edinburgh than in London. His decision to make Bolingbroke's *Craftsman* his political point of departure was, however, particularly appropriate.

The *Craftsman* was founded in 1727, and by 1741 was the longest-lived and most widely read political periodical of the age.[7] Like Hume, Bolingbroke wanted to exploit the resources of the polite periodical press to reshape British politics, but he proposed to do this by creating a new party to oppose Walpole's Whig administration. In his hands politeness was to be a way of encouraging opposition groups to sink their political differences so that they could attack the ministry with new vigour. The *Craftsman* and its celebrated letters on contemporary politics, the 'Dissertation on Parties', were the ideological spearhead of this precarious enterprise. Not only did Bolingbroke have to navigate bitter personal rivalries among leaders of different opposition factions but he had to negotiate profound ideological differences as well. Tories were wedded to maintaining the supremacy of the Anglican Church, and were ambivalent about the legitimacy of the Glorious Revolution and the Hanoverian succession. On the other hand, opposition Whigs tended to be anti-clerical, favouring toleration and believing that the Revolution had established or restored a limited or even elective monarchy. Reconciling such ideological differences was too much for even a highly literate, ingenious and ambitious politician like Bolingbroke, and his 'Dissertation' was more a bravura exercise in skating over thin political ice than a coherent analysis of contemporary politics. In Hume's view, Bolingbroke's influential enterprise was intellectually flawed and politically suspect. It was built around a view of the British constitution which was incoherent and was designed to perpetuate the rage of party rather than end it. As Addison had found a generation before, appeals to moderation did not necessarily encourage moderation in politics.

Bolingbroke's remarks about the constitution touched every political cliché known to his readers. In his view, the English constitution was mixed, part monarchy, part aristocracy and part democracy. It was enshrined in laws, institutions and customs which represented what he cautiously called a 'bargain, a conditional contract between the prince and the people' which had set the terms on which they 'agreed to be governed'. Bolingbroke was carefully noncommittal about its origins – a highly controversial matter. It was enough to say that its principles had been confirmed in Magna Carta and most recently in 1688 by 'a new Magna Charta, from whence new interests, new principles of government, new measures of submission and new obligations arise'.[8] It was the Revolution which had fixed the powers of the king, confirmed the privileges of the people and established, once and for all, that the key to preserving the constitution lay in preserving the independence of parliament from ambitious ministers. This, and the other main principles of the constitution, were, Bolingbroke concluded, 'simple and obvious and fixed as well as any truths can be fixed, in the minds of men, by the most determinate ideas. The state of our constitution then affords an easy and unerring rule, by which to judge of the state of our liberty.'[9]

Bolingbroke's claim that the foundations of the constitution were partly ancient, partly modern, and enshrined in self-evident principles known to every rational citizen formed the framework of his discussion of the political problems of contemporary Britain, and of party in particular. He thought that the origins of the rage of party could be traced back to the reigns of the early Stuarts, although he was systematically evasive about the relationship between these divisions and those of his own time. He was vague about the contentious matter of whether the early Stuarts had attempted to subvert the constitution, as the Whigs believed. What mattered was that they had been singularly imprudent in preaching divine right while indulging 'the excesses of hierarchical and monarchical power' – a mistake the Tudors had always managed to avoid. This imprudence had 'entirely occasioned the miseries which followed'; 'phrenzy provoked phrenzy' both in the Court and in Parliament, and 'all the fury of faction and enthusiasm was employed to destroy the constitution to the very foundations'.[10] Charles ii, James ii and their popish policies had posed new threats to liberty and had led to the formation of a country party in Parliament to defend liberty and religion from Stuart despotism. The Popish Plot and the Exclusion Crisis which had engulfed the political world in the latter years of Charles ii's reign had split this country party and replaced it with Whig and Tory parties which were wedded to impossible ideals of kingship. These two parties had sunk their differences in 1688 in order to depose James ii; this had served as 'a fire, which purged off the dross of both parties', laying the foundations of a new country party composed of moderate men of both persuasions. Indeed, Bolingbroke claimed, it was scarcely proper to call this new party a party at all. 'It is the nation, speaking and acting in the discourse and conduct of particular men', animated by a spirit of liberty inherited from the Saxons and united in supporting the principles of the Glorious Revolution.[11]

And those principles, Bolingbroke thought, were at risk. Corruption was undermining the independence of Parliament and was being defended by the ministry on the preposterous grounds that it was necessary 'to oil the wheels of government, and to render the administration more smooth and easy'. 'Absurd and wicked triflers', Bolingbroke exclaimed, to claim that 'our excellent constitution is no better than a jumble of incompatible powers which would separate and fall to pieces of themselves, unless restrained and upheld by such honourable methods as those of bribery and corruption.'[12] For place, office, pensions and the influence of the Crown generally constituted a new and particularly insidious threat to the mixed constitution, a threat which had been made possible by the growing wealth and influence of the Crown since the Glorious Revolution. Bolingbroke concluded that it was absurd to fight new threats to liberty with old parties which were wedded to outdated ideologies. A new age demanded a new country party to defend the constitution and the only party designations which were – or, rather, ought to be – appropriate in the modern world, were court and country, or, as Bolingbroke put it, anti-constitutionalist and constitutionalist. In Bolingbroke's eyes, the modern patriot was one who was dedicated to destroying an anti-constitutional court party and eradicating corruption in the process.

To Hume, Bolingbroke had stood everything on its head. So far from being a threat to the constitution, party and corruption were an integral part of it. So far from being awkwardly rooted in the gothic and modern worlds, the constitution was modern and unique only in the sense that it was uniquely ill-equipped to secure the liberty and prosperity of modern Britain. Thus Walpole's admittedly grubby machine politics were a function of the constitution and were probably the best Britons could hope for. Bolingbroke's attempt to build a new country party was to be revealed as little more than a specious attempt to keep the rage of party alive in a new form. But how was this message to be conveyed?

In translating the metaphysical language of the *Treatise* into a party political language, Hume had to make it clear that the most 'natural' form of government was one that was simple, not mixed; regular, not uncertain in its operations; and supported by opinion which was shaped by considerations of interest and habit rather than by abstract reasoning about the principles of government. In his essay 'That Politics May Be Reduced to a Science', he laid down the central principles of his political and historical thinking: that the political life of a polity was shaped by its constitution; that the constitutions of mixed monarchies were more prone to faction and civil disorder than simple forms of government; and that hereditary monarchy was to be preferred to elective monarchy, aristocracy or republics, all of which encouraged faction. For civilized polities were governed by laws, not men, and absolute sovereigns whose power was undivided and whose authority was undisputed were more likely to provide regular government and to contain faction and political corruption. 'Good laws', he concluded, 'may beget order and moderation in the government where the manners and customs have instilled little humanity or justice into the tempers of men.'[13] As always, regularity in moral or political behaviour was the key to encouraging the spread of security, happiness and understanding.

But, first of all, Hume had to explain his political thinking to his new readers, an operation he performed with notable iconoclasm. 'All human affairs, are entirely governed by *opinion*,' he wrote.

> It is, therefore, on opinion only that government is founded; and this maxim extends to the most despotic and most military governments, as well as to the most free and most popular. The soldan of Egypt, or the emperor of Rome, might drive his harmless subjects, like brute beasts, against their sentiments and inclination. But he must, at least, have led his *mamelukes* or *praetorian bands*, like men, by their opinion.[14]

For contemporaries, this was alarmingly sceptical thinking; after all, in conventional usage, opinion was fickle, unstable and apt to be corrupted by prejudice, superstition and enthusiasm; as such, it was associated with the fragmentation of moral, political and religious certainties and with the social and political instability that followed. Hume had to show that political opinion was a complicated but explicable phenomenon which could be explained scientifically and systematically. In 'Of the First Principles of Government' he showed that our political thought was compounded of general and particular ideas. Thus we have general opinions about the necessity of government to secure our property and to preserve the public interest and about the best sort of government to perform these tasks. We also have particular opinions about the merits of our own and other peoples' governments. An individual's political thought is thus likely to be a complicated and probably incoherent amalgam of general and particular political opinions. Hume went on to show that different types of political opinion had different characteristics which were likely to influence political behaviour in different ways. Opinions about the public interest required critical thinking about the present interests of society and the best ways of preserving it. When such thinking was found, it was to be respected; when it governed the political thinking of a significant number of citizens, it 'gives great security to any government'.[15] On the other hand opinions about the legitimacy of any dynasty or regime could all too easily become antiquarian and breed 'enthusiasm' – a dangerous tendency evident in Tory and Jacobite infatuation with the rights of the Stuart dynasty, and in Whig infatuation with ideas of an ancient British constitution. And, if a significant number of citizens thought that their property was at risk, it was likely that habits of obedience would fade and that the authority of government would start to crumble. Thus the habit of obedience to existing government was the only power which was strong enough to neutralize the potentially disturbing effects of political debate and secure the authority of government. This subtle and compact account of the principles of political behaviour must have made hard reading for polite audiences. But it had avoided the crudely simplistic assumptions about political behaviour which were beloved of historians then as now. Moreover, it provided the framework for an excellent analysis of political opinion in modern Britain.

Hume's political essays were, first and foremost, about party, and the constitution. Like Bolingbroke he agreed that the constitution had changed since 1688. The wealth and influence of the Crown had certainly increased, upsetting the original balance of the constitution in the process; the question was whether liberty was really in danger. He agreed with modern Whigs that the wealth and power of the Commons had grown at the expense of the Crown and that they could

now 'engross the whole power of the constitution', and turn Britain
into an elective monarchy or even a republic. On the other hand they
had not done so. 'How . . . shall we solve this paradox?' Hume asked.
'And by what means is this member of our constitution confined
within the proper limits, since, for our very constitution, it must necessarily have as much power as it demands, and can only be confined
by itself? How is this consistent with our experience of human
nature?' The question was beautifully put and could be answered
with deceptive simplicity. The Commons had not pressed their advantage because they did not think it was in their interest to do so. Indeed,
it was clear that they were perfectly willing to support the authority
of the Crown provided they had a chance of enjoying its patronage.

> We may, therefore, give to this influence what name we please; we
> may call it by the invidious appellations of *corruption* and *depend-
> ence*; but some degree and some kind of it are inseparable from the
> very nature of the constitution and necessary to the preservation of
> our mixed government.[16]

Thus the growth in the wealth and power of the Crown and Commons had brought about a new balance of power between Crown and
Parliament. No doubt it was a different balance from any that had
existed in the Saxon era, at the time of Magna Carta or even in 1688.
No doubt the power of the Crown would continue to grow, and Bolingbroke was certainly right to argue that England was being led
along the path to absolute monarchy. But what of that? If the Commons tried to turn Britain into an elective monarchy or a republic
once more it would lead to rebellion, civil war and the horrors of a
new military despotism. Surely it was better to submit quietly to the
present government and reflect on ways in which the constitution
could be regularized and perfected in the future – something Hume
himself was to consider in a future essay, 'Of the idea of a Perfect
Commonwealth'. And surely calm reflection would show that there
was a world of difference between an irregular and violent despotism
and the civilized absolute monarchies of the modern age, which were
simple and regular in structure and more 'natural' than the rickety
mixed constitution of Britain.

But though all kinds of government be improved in modern times, yet monarchical government seems to have made the greatest advances towards perfection. It may now be affirmed of civilized monarchies, what was formerly said in praise of republics alone, *that they are a government of Laws, not of Men.* They are found susceptible of order, method, and constancy, to a surprising degree. Property is there secure, industry encouraged, the arts flourish, and the prince lives secure among his subjects, like a father among his children.[17]

In other words, absolute monarchy did not mean arbitrary monarchy, as so many Englishmen thought, and that was why Hume could conclude, mischievously and iconoclastically, 'absolute monarchy, therefore, is the easiest death, the true *Euthanasia* of the British constitution'.[18]

The problem of party and party conflict lay at the heart of the *Essays Moral and Political.* No polite moralist detested party or faction more passionately than Hume, or had a better understanding of its dangers for society and government. No one saw more clearly how confused and confusing men's political thinking could become when circumstances unsettled their habits of obedience to established authority. This was why 'legislators and founders of states, who transmit a system of laws and institutions to secure the peace, happiness, and liberty of future generations', were 'the greatest benefactors of mankind', for good laws and regular government were all that could encourage us to submit quietly to political authority. This was why 'the founders of sects and factions [ought] to be detested and hated; because the influence of faction is directly contrary to that of laws'. He continued,

Factions subvert government, render laws impotent, and beget the fiercest animosities among men of the same nation, who ought to give mutual assistance and protection to each other. And what should render the founders of parties more odious, is the difficulty of extirpating these weeds, when once they have taken root in any state. They naturally propagate themselves for many centuries, and seldom end but by the total dissolution of that government, in which they are sown. They are, besides, plants which grow most plentiful in the richest soil; and though absolute governments be not wholly free from them, it must be confessed, that they rise more easily, and propagate themselves faster in free governments, where they always infect the legislature itself, which alone could be able, by the steady application of rewards and punishments, to eradicate them.[19]

As every contemporary knew, the British party system was exceedingly complicated. Hume began with a theoretical discussion of different types of party, and he concluded that the British system was an amalgam of several types. Some parties had their roots in family feuds and were based on personal loyalty to individuals and families which persisted long after the original cause of the quarrel had been forgotten. Some were based on genuine differences of opinion about the public interest; something that was of particular significance in a country like Britain, which was profoundly divided by geography, economic interest, manners, religion, laws and language. The modern age, however, had spawned a new and particularly insidious type of party in the shape of the party of principle, which appealed to highly abstract conceptions of legitimate political authority; in Britain, this was something closely connected with religion. Hume's political thought made it clear that the character of party politics in any country was determined by its constitution. Thus family feuds were characteristic of the small republics of the ancient and modern world which English opposition Whigs so naively admired and regarded as an appropriate model for a large, modern commercial polity to emulate. In these republics, Hume wrote, political authority was elective and it was all too easy for family feuds to flourish.

> Every domestic quarrel, there, becomes an affair of state. Love, vanity, emulation, any passion, as well as ambition and resentment, begets public division . . . What can be imagined more trivial than the difference between one colour of livery and another in horse races? Yet this difference begat two most inveterate factions in the Greek empire, the PRASINI and VENETI, who never suspended their animosities till they ruined that unhappy government.[20]

In Hume's analysis the enormous, indeed overriding, advantage of absolute monarchies was that sovereign power was undivided and hereditary. Thus kings were able to recognize genuine differences of opinion between the nobility and commons, merchants and land-owners about the public interest and to contain the corrosive power of faction. However, the British constitution was part monarchy and part republic, and it was inevitable that differences of interest would be compounded by genuine differences of opinion about the correct balance that ought to exist between its parts. It was a situation that was bound to foster ideological party divisions.

> The crown will naturally bestow all trust and power upon those whose principles, real or pretended, are more favourable to monarchical gov-ernment; and this temptation will naturally engage them to go greater lengths than their principles would otherwise carry them. Their antagon-ists, who are disappointed in their ambitious aims, throw themselves into the party whose sentiments incline them to be most jealous of royal power, and naturally carry those sentiments to a greater height than sound politics will justify. Thus *Court* and *Country*, which are the gen-uine offspring of the British government, are a kind of mixed parties, and are influenced both by principle and by interest. The heads of the factions are commonly most governed by the latter motive; the inferior members of them by the former.[21]

This put paid to Bolingbroke's claims that his new country party was the only genuine 'constitutionalist' party, and it showed the folly of encouraging his supporters to eradicate a court party that was as much a part of the constitution as his. It also questioned Bolingbroke's assertion that his country party was a by-product of the politics of the later Stuart era. This reopened the question of the nature of the polit-ical divisions that had emerged in the early seventeenth century. In a notably sketchy essay, 'Of the Parties of Great Britain', Hume sug-gested that the origins of the modern party system were to be found in the early seventeenth century, in the reigns of the first two Stuarts. Before then 'the English constitution . . . had lain in a kind of confu-sion, yet so as that the subjects possessed many noble privileges, which, though not exactly bounded and secured by law, were univer-sally deemed, from long possession, to belong to them as their birthright'. Hume was uncharacteristically vague about the nature of these privileges but went on to explain that, by ruling for eleven years without Parliament, Charles I had been foolish enough to revoke them. When constrained by 'necessity' to call a parliament in 1640 he had aroused a spirit of liberty and had set in motion the controversies that created party divisions and precipitated civil war. In Charles II's reign, 'New parties arose, under the appellation of *Whig* and *Tory*, which have continued ever since to confound and distract our government.' These had somehow become encumbered with the abstract sentiments about liberty and authority which gave birth to the Glorious Revolution and had continued to shape party prejudices ever since.[22]

This attempt to explain the origins of the modern constitution and the party system was not a success, and Hume was to replace it with an analysis of incomparably greater power, apologizing to readers of later editions of his essays with a footnote.

> Some of the opinions delivered in these Essays, with regard to the public transactions in the last century, the Author, on more accurate examination, found reason to retract in his History of Great Britain. And as he would not enslave himself to the systems of either party, neither would he fetter his judgement by his own preconceived opinions and principles; nor is he ashamed to acknowledge his mistakes. These mistakes were indeed, at that time, almost universal in this kingdom.[23]

By the time he came to write the *History* Hume had realized that the Tudor constitution was far less confused than he had thought and that Elizabeth's government, arbitrary and even tyrannical though it was, had been obeyed and paradoxically revered by Parliament and people. This discovery only made the plight of the first two Stuarts more puzzling. If Englishmen were fired with a natural love of liberty as so many patriots claimed, why had their behaviour in Elizabeth's reign been so servile? On the other hand, if they were no more than slaves under Elizabeth, why had they lost their respect for arbitrary government under her successors? Somehow, natural habits of obedience to established government had broken down with disastrous results. It was a question which tested Hume's understanding of political behaviour at every level.

By the time he came to write the *History*, Hume had made a second discovery; that the origins of Whig and Tory political thinking could also be traced to the early seventeenth century and to the events which had led to the Civil War. But why had the English adopted a set of highly abstract and arcane political opinions and pursued them with such zeal at a time when no one's property was at risk? Hume brought this question into focus in 1747 in two essays, 'Of the Original Contract' and 'Of Passive Obedience', which were published in the third and last volume of his *Essays Moral and Political*. These essays were designed to show how abstract this political thinking was and how strikingly 'unnatural' by Humean standards. He dealt briskly with Tory ideas of indefeasible right and passive obedience, which, 'by tracing up government to the Deity, endeavour to render it so sacred and inviolate, that it must be little less than sacrilege, however tyrannical it may become, to touch or invade it in the smallest article'.[24] Even if one assumed that God was the source of all political authority, did that mean that every king, tyrant or inferior magistrate, every highwayman or pirate who tried to exert his power over his victims, did so with divine approval and could reasonably expect them to believe that it was sacrilegious to resist? Clearly we obey kings for reasons which are different to those we give for obeying robbers who hold us in their power.

So how was the nature of political consent to be defined? Once again, Hume took the opportunity of translating his metaphysical account of politics into the language of party politics and politeness by launching a full-scale attack on a 'fashionable theory' of the Whigs which Bolingbroke had also tried to appropriate for his new country party. Hume described the 'fashionable theory' like this. In arguing that 'by founding government altogether on the consent of the people, [these politicians suppose] that there is a kind of *original contract*, by which the subjects have tacitly reserved the power of resisting their sovereign, whenever they find themselves aggrieved by that authority which they have for certain purposes, voluntarily intrusted him'.[25] This presupposed that all men in all ages were born in a state of natural equality and that they were capable of entering into formal contractual relations with a sovereign about the terms on which they would surrender their natural liberty to govern themselves. But philosophy and history taught that this image of political man was not only preposterous but dangerous, because it encouraged men to distrust government. For when are we ever in the state of natural equality that the ideologists spoke of? When are we ever free to decide whether or not we should obey government? All history taught that human beings were driven by necessity to submit to whatever form of government offered them protection. If one looked at the evidence of ordinary language one would discover princes 'who claim their subjects as their property, and associate their independent right of sovereignty from conquest or succession' and one would find subjects who take it for granted that they are born under 'obligations of obedience to a certain sovereign, as much as under the ties of reverence and duty to certain parents'.

> These connections are always conceived to be equally independent of our consent, in Persia and China, in France and Spain, and even in Holland and England, wherever the doctrines above mentioned [about contract and resistance] have not been carefully inculcated. Obedience or subjection becomes so familiar, that most men never make any inquiry about its origin or cause, more than about the principle of gravity, resistance, or the most universal laws of nature. Or if curiosity ever move them, as soon as they learn that they themselves and their ancestors have, for several ages, or from time immemorial, been subject to such a form of government or such a family, they immediately acquiesce, and acknowledge their obligation to allegiance. Were you to preach, in most parts of the world, that political connections are founded altogether on voluntary consent or a mutual promise, the magistrate would soon imprison you as seditious for loosening the ties of obedience; if your friends did not before shut you up as delirious, for advancing such absurdities.[26]

As for the notion that government was founded on an original contract which continued to bind subsequent generations, history taught that 'almost all the governments which exist at present, or of which there remains any record in story, have been founded originally, either on usurpation or conquest, or both, without any pretence of a fair consent or voluntary subjection of the people'. And just to make the point crystal clear, Hume focused the argument on the Glorious Revolution.

> Let not the establishment at the Revolution deceive us, or make us so much in love with a philosophical origin to government, as to imagine all others monstrous and irregular. Even that event was far from corresponding to these refined ideas. It was only the succession, and that only in the regal part of government, which was then changed: and it was only the majority of seven hundred, who determined that change for near ten millions. I doubt not, indeed, but the bulk of those ten millions acquiesced willingly in the determination: but was the matter left, in the least, to their choice? Was it not justly supposed to be, from that moment, decided, and every man punished, who refused to submit to the new sovereign? How otherwise could the matter have ever been brought to any issue or conclusion?[27]

Once again Hume presented political man as a creature of habit, whose natural disposition was to submit quietly to established government, who distrusted resistance to political authority, and whose natural allegiance to government was shaken only when he found himself in uncertain circumstances. But that only underlined the extraordinary paradox of seventeenth-century British history. For while it was perfectly easy to understand why ideological differences survived – his discussion of the squabbles between the Prasini and the Veneti over their jockeys' liveries had shown that – it was still necessary to explain their origins and, more particularly, why bizarre opinions about the constitution had been able to destroy a monarchy that had not threatened anyone's life or property. So far as Hume was concerned, religious differences alone had the power to deflect the minds of men from the business of ordinary life and weaken their natural habits of obedience to the point where they were willing to rebel. The political power of religion was a phenomenon that continued to fascinate him as a historian of England, and he laid some of the most important groundwork of his analysis in 1741 in the most remarkable of all his early essays, 'Of Superstition and Enthusiasm'.

'Of Superstition and Enthusiasm' was one of a series of broadsides that Hume fired at the Christian Church and it was to have a profound influence on historians like William Robertson, Edward Gibbon and Sir Walter Scott. Indeed, it is the starting point for nearly all subsequent secular thinking about the history of religion. Its main purpose was to analyse the political implications of religious thought and to show that both superstition and enthusiasm had potentially disastrous consequences for political stability. Psychologically, religious superstition was the natural offspring of 'weakness, fear, melancholy together with ignorance', and that in turn encouraged priestcraft.

> It represents the man to himself in such despicable colours, that he appears unworthy in his own eyes, of aproaching the Divine presence, and naturally has recourse to any other person, whose sanctity of life, or perhaps impudence and cunning, have made him be supposed more favoured by the Divinity. To him the superstitious intrust their devotions: to his care they recommend their prayers, petitions, and sacrifices: and by this means, they hope to render their addresses acceptable to their incensed Deity. Hence the origin of PRIESTS.

Superstition had obvious attractions for princes. It had a natural tendency to 'gradually and insensibly [render] men tame and submissive'. On the other hand, it also had a tendency to turn the priest into 'the tyrant and disturber of human society, by his endless contentions, persecutions, and religious wars', a claim that was to be amply illustrated in the *History*.[28]

The roots of enthusiasm, by contrast, lay in 'hope, pride, presumption, a warm imagination' and, inevitably, the ignorance that Hume always saw as the mother of religious belief. For the enthusiast – and here we see the makings of Hume's later account of English Puritanism and Scottish Presbyterianism –

> Every thing mortal and perishable vanishes as unworthy of attention; and a full range is given to the fancy in the invisible regions, or world of Spirits, where the soul is at liberty to indulge itself in every imagination, which may best suit its present taste and disposition. Hence arise raptures, transports, and surprising flights of fancy; and, confidence and presumption still increasing, these raptures, being altogether unac-

countable, and seeming quite beyond the reach of our ordinary faculties, are attributed to the immediate inspiration of that Divine Being who is the object of devotion. In a little time, the inspired person comes to regard himself as a distinguished favourite of the Divinity; and when this phrensy once takes place, which is the summit of enthusiasm, every whimsey is consecrated: human reason, and even morality, are rejected as fallacious guides; and the fanatic madman delivers himself over, blindly and without reserve, to the supposed illapses of the Spirit, and to inspiration from above.

If superstition bred priestcraft, enthusiasm encouraged a distrust of priests, hierarchy and civil government and was capable of producing 'the most cruel disorders in human history'. In time, however, its ardour was apt to wane and:

> in all fanatical sects, [it sinks] into the greatest remissness and coolness in sacred matters; there being no body of men among them endowed with sufficient authority, whose interest is concerned to support the religious spirit; no rites, no ceremonies, no holy observances, which may enter into the common train of life, and preserve the sacred principles from oblivion.[29]

As Hume might have put it, euthanasia was the fate of dissenting sects.

This astonishing essay, which really needs to be digested whole, was too rich a food for even Hume to digest in 1741. His tentative account of the origin of party had emphasized the political origins of the divisions between court and country that had led to civil war. Thirteen years later, in the first volume of the *History*, these historiographical links with Bolingbroke were to be severed as Hume showed how religious controversy, in the shape of the Arminian superstition of the king's supporters and the enthusiasm of their Puritan opponents, had led to the destruction of the monarchy. By then, Hume had realized that the apocalyptic power of religious enthusiasm was the only force which was capable of destroying men's natural loyalties to a government which they had no other reason to disobey. He had realized that, so far from being a conflict about the constitution, the Civil War had been a war of religion. And he could see that the enduring legacy of the Civil War was not only the modern mixed constitution and the party system which was embedded in it, but the superstition and enthusiasm which continued to fire the ideological abstractions of modern party politics.

Within a year of publishing the *Treatise*, Hume had completed a remarkable analysis of British politics at the end of the Walpolian era in the somewhat visionary hope that it would teach the polite world the principles of politics and the political world the principles of politeness. The polite world had been told that opinion and the horrors of superstition and enthusiasm presented it with political as well as moral problems and that it should begin to think of the virtues of moderation in a political as well as a moral context. But the lessons that had to be learned could hardly have been less palatable. It was necessary to stop judging statesmen by impossible standards, and to realize that they could only be judged as human beings who had to take the political world as they found it and maintain their power as best they could. All that could be hoped was that in time, and with luck, government would become more regular and less prone to faction.

And what did that mean in practice but accepting that the Matchless Constitution was uniquely difficult to manage, that it was the only constitution there was? It was a constitution with a natural tendency to provoke faction, which was bound to give birth to Walpolian managers who would be difficult to admire and difficult to dispense with. Hume's verdict on Walpole, written on the eve of his fall in 1742, foreshadows the cool, disenchanted Tacitean estimates he was to make of a singularly humdrum line of Stuart kings. He was the only sort of statesman the English could expect, the only one they deserved.

> Sir Robert Walpole, Prime Minister of *Great Britain*, is a man of ability, not a genius; good-natured, not virtuous; constant, not magnanimous; moderate, not equitable. His virtues, in some instances, are free from the alloy of those vices which usually accompany such virtues: he is a generous friend, without being a bitter enemy. His vices, in other instances, are not compensated by those virtues which are nearly allied to them: his want of enterprise is not attended with frugality. The pri-

vate character of the man is better than the public: his virtues more than his vices: his fortune greater than his fame. With many good qualities, he has incurred the public hatred: with good capacity, he has not escaped ridicule. He would have been esteemed more worthy of his high station, had he never possessed it; and is better qualified for the second than for the first place in any government; his ministry has been more advantageous to his family than to the public, better for this age than for posterity; and more pernicious by bad precedents than by real grievances. During his time trade has flourished, liberty declined, and learning gone to ruin. As I am a man, I love him; as I am a scholar, I hate him; as I am a *Briton*, I calmly wish his fall. And were I a member of either House, I would give my vote for removing him from St James's; but should be glad to see him retire to *Houghton-Hall*, to pass the remainder of his days in ease and pleasure.[30]

Once Englishmen had learned how to judge their statesmen in this spirit, they would have learned that the modern party system was here to stay. Only then would party rage evaporate; only then would the future of commerce be secure; only then would the British understand their constitution and the true nature of their interests, their liberties and their happiness.

Such lessons could be taught by means of philosophy and political science. But they could be taught more popularly and more entertainingly by means of a new history of England written according to the agenda Hume had developed in these political essays. It was a history which would be focused on the extraordinary and unexpected collapse of political authority that had taken place in the early seventeenth century and had led to civil war. It would involve assessing the role of religion and the rise of the middling ranks in shaping the history of modern Britain. Above all, it would teach the citizens of Walpolian Britain how to judge their rulers.

5

The History of England: I

The Stuarts and the Origins of the Matchless Constitution

By 1747 Hume had finished with contemporary British politics and was turning to history. His outlook on history was classical, polite and above all conventional; after all, if history was to be useful, it had to be read and, if it was to be read, it had to respect generic conventions. Like Addison, Hume thought that 'Those who have succeeded best in [writing history], are such, who, beside their natural Good Sense and Learning, have themselves been versed in publick Business, and thereby acquired a thorough Knowledge of Men and Things.'[1] And that, as well as a salary, was why Hume agreed to join General St Clair as his secretary on a military mission to the court of Turin in 1747. He told a friend,

> I shall have an opportunity of seeing Courts & Camps; & if I can afterwards, be so happy as to attain leizure and other opportunities, this knowledge may even turn to account to me, as a man of letters, which I confess has always been the sole object of my ambition. I have long had an intention, in my riper years, of composing some History; & I question not but some greater experience of the Operations of the Field, & the Intrigues of the Cabinet, will be requisite, in order to enable me to speak with judgement upon these subjects.[2]

The classical commonplace that those who were best suited to write about public affairs were those who had experience of them had its roots in a culture that believed that history should be written for the edification of the great. In a polite age, however, it was perfectly reasonable to think that it should be written for the middling ranks. Nor did Hume forget that these included 'my female readers', who ought to be rescued from *petites histoires* in favour of history written on Machiavellian principles. For Machiavelli had used history to teach the principles of prudence by setting statesmen and politicians in their contexts and judging their conduct accordingly. Indeed history seemed particularly well suited to teaching morality in the modern age.

> When a man of business enters into life and action, he is more apt to consider the characters and actions of men, as they stand in themselves; and has his judgement warped on every occasion by the violence of his passion. When a philosopher contemplates characters and manners in his closet, the general abstract view of the objects leaves the mind so cold and unmoved, that the sentiments of nature have no room to play, and he scarce feels the difference between vice and virtue. History keeps in a just medium between these extremes, and places objects in their true point of view. The writers of history, as well as the readers, are sufficiently interested in the characters and events, to have a lively sentiment of blame or praise: and, at the same time, have no particular interest or concern to pervert their judgement.[3]

But the business of placing objects in their true point of view was far from straightforward. It meant viewing government and politics in the light of the problems involved in defending the constitution, teaching readers to think of constitutions as political rather than legal arrangements, and encouraging them to judge their rulers on their success in enforcing the rules of justice on which the preservation of life, property and the constitution depended. In other words, it meant teaching readers to think about the constitution and government in the light of changing historical circumstances and those changes in the distribution of property on which the progress of civilization depended. That is, it meant taking account of the fact that the British constitution, like any other, was in a state of continual flux.

Hume had already begun to think of the demands of writing the history of civilization in the *Essays Moral and Political*, where he had reflected on the effects of regular government in Europe on manners, morals and the progress of the arts and sciences, and he was to develop these interests while he was on tour with General St Clair.

He undertook an intensive reading of the classics, studied Montesquieu's epoch-making *Spirit of the Laws* (1748) and corresponded with its author, and it has been suggested that he even contemplated writing a history of civilization in antiquity.[4] Be that as it may, it is clear that by 1748 Hume was clearing the ground for a history of his own country. With the publication of the two *Enquiries* of 1748 and 1751 and the *Political Discourses* of 1752, his outstanding philosophical commitments were complete. His appointment as Librarian of the Advocates' Library in Edinburgh in 1752 gave him access to one of the largest libraries in Britain. His first plans were for a three-volume history of the House of Stuart. The first volume would begin with the reign of James I and conclude with the execution of Charles I, the second would run from the history of the Commonwealth and Protectorate to the Revolution of 1688, and the third would cover the remaining period to the death of Queen Anne and the accession of the Hanoverian dynasty, 'for I dare come no nearer the present times' Hume confessed to a friend in 1753.[5] *The History of Great Britain Volume i. Containing the Reigns of James I and Charles I* was published in 1754.

Starting with the Stuarts rather than the Tudors had not been a particularly easy decision. As he told Adam Smith

> I confess, I was once of the same Opinion with you & thought that the best period to begin an English History was about Henry the 7th. But you will please to observe, that the Change, which then happen'd in public Affairs, was very insensible, and did not display its Influence till many Years afterwards. Twas under James that the House of Commons began first to raise their Head, & then the Quarrel betwixt Privilege & Prerogative commenc'd. The Government, no longer opprest by the enormous Authority of the Crown, display'd its Genius; and the Factions, which then arose, having an Influence on our present Affairs, form the most curious, interesting, & instructive Part of our History.[6]

In other words, the history of the early Stuarts was where the intellectual excitement lay, and this first volume was and remains central to Hume's enterprise. Although much of his thinking about the *longue durée* of British history and the antecedents of the catastrophe that overtook the Stuart monarchy had to be cramped into sketchy digressions and appendices, 'the philosophical spirit which I have so much indulg'd in all my writing, finds here ample Materials to work upon'.[7] It began a revolution in British historical thinking that would be completed ten years and six volumes later. Only then would it be possible to streamline the whole vast enterprise and republish it as a self-standing and integrated work.

The technical problems of writing early-seventeenth-century British history were complicated and multifarious and stemmed from an abundance of newly discovered material and from the polemical uses to which party propagandists had put it. The lapsing of the Licensing Act of 1695 had resulted in a spate of memoirs and accounts of recent history which had culminated in the publication in 1702 of Clarendon's masterpiece, *The History of the Rebellion and the Civil Wars in England*, a work which had transformed contemporaries' understanding of the Civil War and Interregnum and served as the foundation stone of Hume's and every other history. It was the work of a royalist of unimpeachable integrity and intelligence who had participated in many of the events he described and who had been repaid for his devotion to the royalist cause by dismissal and disgrace which he did not deserve. It was a richly documented, authoritative and Olympian apology for the Church and the royal prerogative which had evoked universal admiration from political friend and foe and was, in Hume's opinion, 'the most candid account of those times, composed by any contemporary author'.[8]

But towering above these, rivalling only Clarendon in its importance for shaping Britons' understanding of the disasters of the early seventeenth century, was the work of the French Huguenot Anglophile Paul Rapin de Thoryas, whose monumental *History of England* had been written to explain the English to foreigners and began to appear in 1725. Rapin thought that it was impossible to write an impartial history of England. 'The same Parties are still in being with the same Prejudices [as in James I's time],' he wrote, and histories were always the work of party men.[9] Nevertheless, he achieved a reputation for impartiality by the simple expedient of suspending judgement wherever it mattered. Civil and ecclesiastical history were treated separately. Different sides in different arguments were set out in full with minimal comment, so that readers could draw their own conclusions and every party hack could make whatever use of the material he wanted. It had allowed Bolingbroke and the *Craftsman* to prove that the roots of the constitution were ancient and the ministerial press to prove that they were modern. Optimists even thought that Rapin could be called upon as an advocate of republican government, even of Presbyterianism.[10]

Hume wrote his *History of England* as a polite man of letters who knew the importance of gearing his history to interpretations that would be well known to his readers and could be treated by him critically and philosophically. This was why he told a friend,

> that he never could compose history from manuscript, always preferring exclusively printed authority and books, to which he could attribute impartiality or an approach to it; but certainly . . . he weighed without prejudice, or it may be safely said without the consciousness of it, the authorities which he consulted on both sides, and the probable conclusion which the nature of man, the experience of ages, and the conduct of political men during those ages warranted his drawing.[11]

In other words, he had to discover how to write history that was proof against the politicians and would enable readers to exercise their judgement on philosophical rather than ideological grounds. He greatly admired the fast-moving narrative of events for which Tacitus was so famous and, in France, he would even come to be known as the English Tacitus. More important than Tacitus, however, was Livy, whose closely textured and equally swift account of the decline of the Roman Republic had formed the basis of Machiavelli's *Discourses on the First Decade of T. Livy*. Both works, Livy's and Machiavelli's, were still regarded as classics of political and historical science. They both drew on the principles of human nature in order to analyse the causes of the decline of the Roman Republic and the rise of the Empire and they both expected their readers to reflect on the problems of preserving liberty in a free polity. This programme was particularly attractive to Hume. Not only was it a familiar model which would be understood by his readers, but his own story of the origins of the British constitution had distinctively Livian characteristics as well. For whereas most of his contemporaries thought of the constitutional crises of the seventeenth century as a struggle to preserve an ancient constitution from Stuart despots or from the fanaticism of Puritan zealots, Hume was about to tell the story of the decline and fall of the Elizabethan constitution and the rise of another which had made Britain great and wealthy but which seemed to contain the seeds of its own destruction.

Hume's account of the process by which the authority of the Elizabethan monarchy was eroded and the seeds of the modern constitution were sown is so closely argued and so intelligent that it is well worth following in some detail. His story began with the accession of James I in 1603. 'The Crown of England was never transmitted from father to son with greater tranquillity', he wrote, 'than when it passed from the family of Tudor to that of Stuart.' Heredity, the wishes of the Queen and hopes that James would rule the English with the 'moderation and wisdom' he had shown in Scotland all ensured that he received the unquestioning allegiance of his new subjects. It was a case of an apparently prudent king coming peacefully into his inheritance. From the very first, however, James's prudence was in question. No doubt it was sensible enough to give way to his ministers who wanted to support the rebellious Dutch against the Spanish '[sacrificing] to politics his sense of justice; a quality, which, even when erroneous, is respectable as well as rare in a monarch'. On the other hand, his first encounters with Puritan divines were imprudent in the extreme. Unlike Elizabeth, who refused to discuss religion with her subjects, James did so publicly and with relish at the Hampton Court conference of 1603, beginning the long and fatal process of drawing religion into politics which was to culminate in the catastrophe of civil war. Worst of all was his first encounter with Parliament in 1604, in which he told the Commons that he alone was the author of their privileges, 'a sentiment', Hume remarked, 'which from her conduct, it is certain, that [Elizabeth] had also entertained, and which was the reigning principle of her courtiers and ministers, and the spring of all her administration'. But it was one which she had been wise enough not to put into words.[12]

But what exactly made this conduct *imprudent*? By the time
Hume had completed his history of the Tudors, the answer would be
clear. Here, he was able only to sketch in an argument that was complicated and subtle and must have made difficult reading for all but
a handful of his readers. James's imprudence stemmed from two
sources; he had misunderstood the nature of the English constitution and he had misunderstood the changes which were being
brought about by the progress of society and their political significance. And, while it was hard to sympathize with James's lack of
constitutional sense, it was equally hard to blame him for not understanding profound historical changes which could only be properly
understood with hindsight. James realized that the Elizabethan
monarchy was 'simple and unmixed'. On the other hand, he failed to
realize that the Tudors' power rested upon *opinions*, rather than on
military power, wealth or patronage. That opinion was highly complex. Elizabethans thought of the Queen's authority as 'almost
absolute and unlimited, sacred and indefeasible'. They saw Parliament as little more than 'the ornament of the fabric, without being
in any degree essential to its being and existence'. And while the
Crown's authority was, 'in the judgement of all, not exactly limited;
[it was] in the judgement of some not limitable'. Thus the Tudor
monarchy was not only simple but irregular in structure and the
precise nature of the power of the sovereign was shrouded in mys-
tery. 'For this reason, we need not wonder, that the princes of that
line were so extremely jealous of their prerogative; being sensible,
that, when those claims were ravished from them, they possesed no
influence, by which they could maintain their dignity, or support the
laws.'[13]

What made the problem so delicate was that opinion was shifting. With the growth of luxury and commerce in the sixteenth
century 'arts and industry of all kinds received a mighty encrease;
and elegance in every enjoyment of life became better known and
more cultivated among all ranks of people'. Princes demanded more
sumptuous courts to support their dignity and superiority. Their
counsellors demanded higher taxation to pay for it at a time when
subjects were 'begetting a spirit of freedom and independence' which

made them suspicious of royal authority.[14] For luxury and commerce had destroyed baronial power, and released the gentry from their feudal dependence. This new class of commons was so wealthy that it represented much of the property of Britain. Once again, Hume found himself pointing out that there was nothing to stop the Commons of the Jacobean age from destroying the monarchy altogether if they wanted to do so. Indeed, that is what they were to do in the reign of Charles I.

James understood none of this. He did not realize that he needed military power and patronage to maintain his authority. He ascribed 'that power, almost unlimited, which had been exercised for above a century . . . solely to royal birth and title; not to the prudence and spirit of the monarchs, nor to the conjunctures of the times'.[15] And instead of trying to attach the Commons to the Court by teaching them the joys of 'the softer and more civilized life of the city' he was wont to dispatch them to their country seats,

> where, he hoped, they would bear a more submissive reverence to his authority, and receive less support from each other. But the contrary effect soon followed. The riches, amassed during their residence at home, rendered them independant. Their influence, acquired by hospitality, made them formidable. They would not be led by the court: They could not be driven: And thus the system of the English government received a *total* and a sudden alteration in the course of less than forty years.[16] [*My italics*]

This is the most subtle and sophisticated historical reasoning. As we would expect from the author of the *Treatise* and the *Essays Moral and Political*, constitutional history had been set in a political, not a legal framework and was focused on James's problems in maintaining his authority in a world of shifting opinion which would have to be manipulated if it were to be mastered, and mastered if it were not to destroy government entirely. The tone of Hume's discussion suggests that he too was attempting to manipulate opinion, and it is worth glancing briefly at the historiographical contexts in which he shaped the first, crucial stage of his *History*. It was Rapin who had put the Elizabethan monarchy at the centre of the historiographical stage. He was firmly convinced of the antiquity of the mixed English monarchy and his history was designed to show that the country had been peaceful and prosperous only when Crown and Parliament lived in harmony. Thus wise Parliaments had respected the prerogatives of the king and wise kings had respected the ancient privileges of Parliament. Elizabeth had been the wisest of rulers and, under her rule, the English had been 'the happiest people under the sun'.

> They saw no designs upon their liberties, nor any infringement of thier privileges encouraged. Justice was administered impartially, and the Revenue of the Crown, & the Subsidies granted by Parliament for the publick occasions, were not idly consumed. They had, therefore reason to think the Queen truely loved them, since she caused them to enjoy so great happiness.[17]

James's troubles had stemmed from his attempt to overthrow the mixed constitution. He had proclaimed that he ruled by divine right, and that Parliament owed its privileges to his will alone, a novel and abstract theory, Rapin thought. Thus the Civil War was the result of an attempt by James I and Charles I to subvert the constitution; the king, not the Commons, had been responsible for the disasters of the seventeenth century. That view was highly contentious, not least because it was adopted by Bolingbroke and the Tory party. For a Jacobite High-Church Anglican like Thomas Carte, it was absurd to claim that James had merely invented the theory of divine right. Both he, Elizabeth and their ancestors and successors owed their authority to divine right and the passive obedience of their subjects. The cause of James's troubles lay with the Puritans, who distrusted monarchy and were bent on destroying the Church of England. Indeed, Carte's main criticism of Elizabeth and the early Stuarts was that they had failed to nip the cancer of Puritanism in the bud.[18] But that view differed again from that of historically minded ministerial propagandists who had little time for Tories or Jacobites. Thus Lord Hervey did not believe that there had been a free constitution of any sort before the Restoration of 1660; the earlier history of England had simply been the story of a procession of tyrants, some regal, some baronial, some ecclesiastical, who had ruled without any regard to liberty. No doubt Elizabeth's had been a 'great and glorious' reign, but it was one 'where the People enjoy'd the least Shadow of Liberty'. She had governed in the public interest, but 'absolutely without their consent'. For 'never were the Reins of Prerogative held with a stricter Hand, or the Yoke of Slavery faster bound upon the People's Necks than at this Period of Time'. Thus Elizabeth was the unwitting author of the early Stuarts' misfortunes.

> For these Princes imagining they had a Right to keep up the Prerogative at the Mark they found it, thought of nothing but their Prerogative, and vainly imagin'd the Nation would submit to the same Stretch of the Prerogative when exercised to their Infamy and Ruin, under which it had been acquir'd when employ'd for their Glory and Prosperity.[19]

It is fascinating to read these early chapters of the *History* as the first stage in Hume's reconstruction of British historiographical culture. His analysis was that of a ministerial Whig who believed that the origins of liberty in Britain were modern. But it was a philosophical Whiggery bent on playing off the crude anti-intellectualism of ministerial propagandists against the intellectual strengths of opposition historiography. The end product was a view of the Jacobean and Elizabethan monarchy in which party historiographical prejudices had been refined philosophically to create a more impartial, more polite framework for a history of England.

This was the starting point for Hume's discussion of the central crisis of James's reign, his disagreement with the Commons over Spain which came to a head in the parliament of 1620. It was this that led the Commons to take 'the bold step, unprecedented in England for many years', of attacking every aspect of royal government and even the prerogative itself. It was this that led the King to reply that the privileges of the Commons were dependent solely on his will. This reply provoked the Commons' famous retort that their privileges were 'the ancient and undoubted birth-right and inheritance of the subjects of England'. And it was this that led to that fateful and dramatic moment in which the King tore the protestation out of the journal of the House of Commons.

> The king having thus, with so rash and indiscreet a hand, torn off that sacred veil, which had hitherto covered the English constitution, and

which threw an obscurity upon it, so advantageous to royal prerogative, every man began to indulge himself in political reasonings and enquiries; and the same factions, which commenced in parliament, were propagated throughout the nation.[20]

Thus 'were first regularly formed, though without acquiring these denominations, the parties of court and country; parties, which have ever since continued, and which, while they oft threaten the total dissolution of the government, are the real causes of its permanent life and vigour'.[21] They were founded on two sets of principles, or *mentalités*, and it was these that eventually gave birth to that peculiarly English phenomenon, the mixed constitution.

Hume's account of the political thinking that gave rise to theories of divine right and of original contract was of great subtlety and was designed to show how abstract opinions about sovereignty could be distilled out of the sort of political disputes he had described.

All history, said the partizans of the court, as well as the history of England, justify the king's position with regard to the origin of popular privileges; and every reasonable man must allow, that, as monarchy is the most simple form of government, it must first have occurred to rude and uninstructed mankind. The other complicated and artificial additions were the successive invention of sovereigns and legislators; or, if they were obtruded on the prince by seditious subjects, their origin must appear, on that very account, still more precarious and unfavourable. In England, the authority of the king, in all the exterior forms of government and in the common style of law, appears totally absolute and sovereign; nor does the real spirit of the constitution, as it has ever discovered itself in practice, fall much short of these appearances. The parliament is created by his will; by his will it is dissolved. It is his will alone, though at the desire of both houses, which gives authority to laws. To all foreign nations, the majesty of the monarch seems to merit sole attention and regard. And no subject, who has exposed himself to royal indignation, can hope to live with safety in the kingdom; nor can he even leave it, according to law, without the consent of his master. If a magistrate, invironed with such power and splendor, should consider his authority as sacred, and regard himself as the annointed of heaven, his pretensions may bear a very favourable construction. Or, allowing them to be merely pious frauds, we need not be surprized, that the same stratagem which was practised by Minos, Numa, and the most celebrated legislators of antiquity, should now, in these restless and inquisitive times, be employed by the king of England. Subjects arc not raised above that quality, though assembled in parliament. The same respect and deference is still due to their prince. Though he indulges them in the privilege of laying before him their domestic grievances, with which they are supposed to be best acquainted, this warrants not their bold intrusion into every province of government. And to all judicious examiners, it must appear, 'That the lines of duty are as much transgressed by a more independent and less respectful exercise of acknowledged powers, as by the usurpation of such as are new and unusual.'[22]

This meticulous analysis of a court *mentalité* was followed by that of the 'lovers of liberty'. They reasoned from quite different premises:

It is vain, said they, that the king traces up the English government to its first origin, in order to represent the privileges of parliament as dependent and precarious: Prescription and the practice of so many ages, must, long ere this time, have given a sanction to these assemblies, even though they had been derived from an origin no more dignified, than that which he assigns them. If the written records of the English nation, as asserted, represent parliaments to have risen from the consent of monarchs, the principles of human nature, when we trace government a step higher, must show us, that monarchs themselves owe all their authority to the voluntary submission of the people. But, in fact, no age can be shown, when the English government was altogether an unmixed monarchy. And if the privileges of the nation have, at any period, been overpowered by violent irruptions of foreign force or domestic usurpation; the generous spirit of the people has ever seized the first opportunity of re-establishing the ancient government and constitution. Though in the style of the laws, and in the usual forms of administration, royal authority may be represented as sacred and supreme; whatever is essential to the exercise of sovereign and legislative power, must still be regarded as equally divine and inviolable. Or, if any distinction be made in this respect, the preference is surely due to those national councils, by whose interposition the exorbitancies of tyrannical power are restrained, and that sacred liberty is preserved, which heroic spirits, in all ages, have deemed more precious than life itself. Nor is it sufficient to say, that the mild and equitable administration of James, affords little occasion, or no occasion of complaint. How moderate soever the exercise of his prerogative, how exact soever his observance of the laws and constitution; if he founds his authority on arbitrary and dangerous principles, it is requisite to watch him with the same care, and to oppose him with the same vigour, as if he had indulged himself in all the excesses of cruelty and tyranny.[23]

Here, then, were two sets of opinions, two *mentalités*, which were shaping and sharpening political divisions in James's kingdom. And, as each set of opinions excluded the other, their natural tendency was to encourage conflict.

The turbulent government of England, ever fluctuating between privilege and prerogative, would afford a variety of precedents, which might be pleaded on both sides. In such delicate questions, the people must be divided: The arms of the state were still in their hands: A civil war must ensue; a civil war, where no party or both parties would justly bear the blame, and where the good and virtuous would scarcely know what vows to form; were it not that liberty, so necessary to the perfection of human society, would be sufficient to byass their affections towards the side of its defenders.[24]

This deeply divided political culture was James's disastrous legacy to his son. In Hume's final analysis, he was no despot intent on overthrowing an ancient constitution but an imprudent ruler of limited talents who was out of his depth. His virtues were marred by commonplace vices; generosity by extravagance, learning by pedantry, wisdom by cunning, a pacific disposition by cowardice and friendship by 'light fancy and boyish fondness'. In his efforts to earn the good will of all 'he was able to preserve fully the esteem and regard of none. His capacity was considerable; but fitter to discourse on general maxims than to conduct any intricate business.' His intentions were good, Hume observed, concluding with the deadly faint praise he reserved for so many of the humdrum line of kings and statesmen that had governed England, but they were 'more adapted to the conduct of private life, than to the government of kingdoms'.[25]

Rapin had presented the Commons as constitutionalists attempting to defend an ancient constitution. Hume had presented them as a wealthy, potentially powerful class, newly released from a state of feudal dependence and in search of a political identity, their behaviour characterized by a mixture of servility and independence, rusticity and zealotry. So far, he had provided a sketch of a class rather than a portrait, and it needed his later volumes to give it substance. Nevertheless, he had cleared the ground for a demonstration of the power of religion to undermine men's natural habits of obedience to established authority, and to turn a new class into a revolutionary one.

Hume's Charles I came to the throne in 1625 as a young, well-meaning, inexperienced ruler with a disastrous taste for ecclesiastics. It was his misfortune to be faced by a Commons which was dominated by a shrewd and purposeful Puritan party soaked in 'the rigid tenets of that sect' and led by men who, for all their intelligence and experience, 'could not enjoy any peace of mind, because obliged to hear prayers offered up to the Divinity, by a priest covered with a white linen vestment'. Their ambition was not to destroy the monarchy, as Jacobites thought, but simply to define the privileges of the people and 'to secure them by firmer and more precise barriers than the constitution had hitherto provided for them'. Their intention was to exploit the financial problems of an inexperienced king. 'The end, they esteemed beneficent and noble: The means, regular and constitutional.'[26] Their campaign, which began in 1625, reached its climax in 1628 in the Petition of Right. The Commons had intended to place limitations on the prerogative in order to preserve a supposedly ancient constitution. In Hume's view, however, the Petition was nothing less than an attempt to overturn a simple monarchy and replace it with a mixed monarchy in which power was divided between the Crown and Parliament. Thus the King's reluctant consent to the Petition was a momentous event in English history, sanctioning 'such a change in the government, as was almost equivalent to a revolution'.[27]

The Matchless Mixed Constitution, in other words, was not the invention of Saxon legislators; it was the work of a party of Puritan zealots whose minds had been shaped by the peculiar political circumstances of the age, and who had little understanding of what they were about. And so far from being the best of all possible constitutions for maintaining government, it was perfectly designed to encourage misunderstanding and conflict. Only the greatest prudence on the part of Crown and Commons would ensure that the new constitution would survive.

None of this was understood by the Commons, whose political judgement had been fatally corrupted by that 'enthusiastic fire, which afterwards set the whole nation in combustion'. No sooner had the Petition of Right been signed by the King than they set about destroying the constitution they had just created. 'Enquiries and debates concerning tonnage and poundage went hand in hand with these theological and metaphysical controversies', and 'to impartial spectators surely, if any such had been at that time in England, it must have given a great entertainment, to see a popular assembly, enflamed with faction and enthusiasm, pretend to discuss questions, to which the greatest philosophers, in the tranquillity of retreat, had never hitherto been able to find any satisfactory solution'. Worst of all, Puritan enthusiasm had so deepened the Commons' distrust of royal authority that they attempted to impose new limitations which would have altogether destroyed the new constitutional arrangements contained in the Petition of Right. As Hume concluded, they could have turned the King into 'a magistrate of a very different nature from any of his predecessors, [who] must fall into a total dependence on subjects, over whom former kings, especially those immediately preceeding, had exercised an authority almost unlimited'. It was this that led Charles to dissolve Parliament in 1629 and to institute the Eleven Years Tyranny, beloved of eighteenth-century historians as the high-water mark of Stuart despotism.[28]

Hume saw the Tyranny as an understandable if chancy response to the crisis provoked by the Commons. No doubt it could be justified as a means of preserving the authority of government but it was a regime that 'still wants somewhat of being entirely legal, and perhaps more of being entirely prudent'.[29] However, he agreed with

Clarendon and Thomas Carte that arbitrary government had not made England rebellious.

> The grievances, under which the English laboured, when considered in themselves, without regard to the constitution, scarcely deserve the name; nor were they either burthensome on the people's properties, or anywise shocking to the natural humanity of mankind. Even the imposition of ship-money, independent of the consequences, was a great and evident advantage to the public; by the judicious use, which the king made of the money levied by that expedient. And though it was justly apprehended, that such precedents, if patiently submitted to, would end in a total disuse of parliaments, and in the establishment of arbitrary authority; Charles dreaded no opposition from the people, who are not commonly much affected with consequences, and require some striking motive, to engage them in a resistance of established government. All ecclesiastical affairs were settled by law and uninterrupted precedent; and the church was become a considerable barrier to the power, both legal and illegal, of the crown. Peace too, industry, commerce, opulence; nay, even justice and lenity of administration, notwithstanding some very few exceptions: All these were enjoyed by the people; and every other blessing of government, except liberty, or rather the present exercise of liberty and its proper security.[30]

This analysis made it clear that, radical though Puritan thought might be, it was not yet the revolutionary force that could overthrow the monarchy. What is more, it was by no means clear what interest the Commons could have in overthrowing a monarchy which did not jeopardize their lives or property. It was this that led Hume to conclude that only religious enthusiasm in its most militant form could break men's natural habits of obedience and turn dissatisfaction into rebellion. The paradox was that this force was unleashed by the King himself, by encouraging the Arminian or High-Church policies of Archbishop Laud.

This was a splendidly polemical conclusion as well as a philosophically interesting one. Like Hume, Carte blamed the Civil War on Puritan enthusiasm and its natural aversion to monarchy, and he thought that Laud's government of the Church had been well designed to root out Puritanism from a Church which had become disgracefully lax. But Hume loathed Laud and thought he bore a heavy responsibility for Charles's downfall. His bigotry was unremitting; he was rash, imprudent and ill-mannered. 'He was in this respect happy, that all his enemies were also imagined by him the declared enemies to loyalty and true piety, and that every exercise of his anger, by that means, became in his eyes a merit and a virtue. This was the man who acquired so great an ascendant over Charles, and who led him, by the facility of his temper, into a conduct which proved so fatal to himself and to his kingdoms.'[31] Hume's account of Laud's Arminian experiment is so understated that only readers of his essay 'Of Superstition and Enthusiasm' would have been in a position to grasp the full implications of his devastating appraisal of Laud's religious policies. As always, what mattered to Hume were the *political* implications of religion. Arminianism had not only exalted the power of king and clergy; it had also enabled the clergy to '[encroach] themselves, on the royal rights the most incontestable; in order to exalt the hierarchy, and procure to their own order dominion and independence'. Thus the natural tendency of Arminian superstition was, paradoxically, the same as that of the Puritan enthusiasts, to undermine the authority of civil government and to turn England into a polity in which politics was at the mercy of priestcraft and directed to the pursuit of 'ghostly' rather than secular concerns. And, absurdly, Charles, 'though extremely jealous of every claim in popular assemblies, seemed rather to encourage than repress those encroachments of his clergy'.[32] The Tyranny had been hijacked by priestcraft and this was its undoing.

If it was imprudent of the King to introduce Arminian superstition into a suspicious Puritan country like England, it was folly to impose it on a naturally rebellious country like Scotland, whose Presbyterian religion was of the most enthusiastic sort. The effects were disastrous.

> All men . . . began to unite and to encourage each other, in opposition
> to the religious innovations introduced into the kingdom. Petitions to
> the council were signed and presented by persons of the highest quality:
> The women took part, and, as was usual, with violence: The clergy,
> every where, loudly declaimed against popery and the liturgy, which
> they represented as the same: The pulpits resounded with vehement

invectives against antichrist: and the populace, who first opposed the service, was often compared to Balaam's ass, an animal, in itself, stupid and senseless, but whose mouth had been opened by the Lord, to the admiration of the whole world. In short, fanaticism mingling with faction, private interest with the spirit of liberty, symptoms appeared, on all hands, of the most dangerous insurrection and disorder.[33]

By 1638 Scottish politics had been engulfed by religion. Civil government was dominated by a clergy nurtured in the spirit of Presbyterian enthusiasm and committed to the destruction of royal authority in order to preserve the Church. Their enthusiasm had broken the natural habits of obedience of the people, who now believed that the 'highest raptures' were 'extasies of devotion' which 'consecrated, in a manner, every individual . . . [by bestowing] a character on him, much superior to what forms and ceremonies could confer'. Charles was now faced by 'a combination of the whole kingdom' which took to arms to defend their Church and defeated the King in the course of two Bishops' Wars in 1639–40.

> Never did refined Athens so exult in diffusing the sciences and liberal arts over a savage world; never did generous Rome so please herself in the view of law and order established by her victorious arms; as the Scots now rejoiced, in communicating their barbarous zeal and theological fervour, to the neighbouring nations.[34]

The Bishops' Wars forced the King to call a parliament to pay off the victorious Scottish armies. But revolutionary Scottish enthusiasm had spread to England and was infecting Parliament. The Long Parliament, which met in 1640, was filled with rustic, independently minded gentry 'who came into Parliament with all their native prejudices about them, and whom the Crown had no means of influencing'. These 'stubborn patriots' had drunk deep of 'the intoxicating poison' of Scottish enthusiasm; they were led by men who regarded any compromise with the Crown as 'slavish dependence' or 'servile flattery'; and they set about dismantling the royal prerogative.[35]

> From the reports of their committees, the house daily passed votes, which mortified and astonished the court, and inflamed and animated

the nation. Ship-money was declared illegal and arbitrary; the sentence against Hambden [*sic*] cancelled; the court of York abolished; compositions for knighthood stigmatized; the enlargement of the forests condemned; patents for monopolies annulled; and every late measure of administration treated with reproach and obloquy. To day, a sentence of the star-chamber was exclaimed against: To morrow, a decree of the high commission. Every discretionary act of council was represented as arbitrary and tyrannical; and the general inference was still inculcated, that a formed design had been laid to subvert the laws and constitution of the kingdom.[36]

By 1642 the constitution had been changed 'in a moment, from a monarchy almost absolute, to a pure democracy'. 'You have taken the whole machinery of government in pieces,' exclaimed the King.[37]

For English republicans this was the moment which saw the birth of a new spirit of liberty and the origins of a glorious republican experiment. But how different Pym, Hampden and Vane were from Cato, Brutus and Cassius!

What a difference, when the discourse, conduct, conversation, and private as well as public behaviour, of both are inspected! Compare only one circumstance, and answer its consequences. The leisure of those noble ancients was totally employed in the study of Grecian eloquence and philosophy; in the cultivation of polite letters and civilized society: The whole discourse and language of the moderns were polluted with mysterious jargon, and full of the lowest and most vulgar hypocrisy.[38]

In England, as in Scotland, politics was being overwhelmed by religion and it needed only an 'indiscretion' to precipitate a catastrophe. It was the King's disastrous attempt to arrest the five leading Puritan members of the Commons in 1642 'to which all the ensuing disorders and civil wars ought immediately and directly to be ascribed'.[39] By now the situation was beyond the control of even the most prudent monarch. A civil war had become inevitable.

This moment marks the climax of the *History of the Stuarts*, and the subsequent account of the Civil War and of the trial and execution of the King reads as the inevitable consequence of a political catastrophe. In his memorable and notorious portrait of the sufferings of

Charles I, Hume called down the wrath of Whig, Tory and Jacobite alike for refusing to present him as a despot or as an Anglican martyr, and for investing his conduct with a certain sentimental stoic dignity. In Hume's eyes, Charles was a martyr only to history, a decent mediocrity belatedly ennobled by glimmerings of understanding of disasters which he was powerless to prevent.

> History, the great mistress of wisdom, furnishes examples of all kinds; and every prudential, as well as moral precept, may be authorized by those events, which her enlarged mirror is able to present to us. From the memorable revolutions, which passed in England during this period, we may naturally deduce the same useful lesson, which Charles himself, in his later years, inferred; that it is dangerous for princes, even from the appearance of necessity, to assume more authority, than the laws have allowed them. But, it must be confessed, that these events furnish us with another instruction, no less natural, and no less useful, concerning the madness of the people, the furies of fanaticism, and the danger of mercenary armies.[40]

The history of the later Stuart era was written surprisingly quickly and was published in 1756, only two years after the first volume. It is arrestingly organized, beginning and ending with revolution. The first, which began in 1649 with the execution of the King, had brought about the dissolution of government, threatened the dissolution of society and concluded with the military despotism of Oliver Cromwell. Hume thought that the Glorious Revolution of 1688 had left Britain teetering on the edge of a similar disaster from which she had been saved only by good luck, in the shape of James II's sudden flight from England, and by the remarkable political sagacity of William of Orange. For Hume, the Interregnum had been an awful warning of what could happen to a country with a mixed constitution and he was only cautiously optimistic that it would not happen again.

Hume's account of the Interregnum was terse and memorable. With the 'murder' of the King, the constitution collapsed and 'from tranquillity, concord, submission, sobriety, [the English nation] passed in an instant to a state of faction, fanaticism, rebellion and almost frenzy'. Speculative opinions about new republics and new forms of religion abounded. The Levellers, '[disdaining] all dependence and subordination', called for an equal distribution of property. The Fifth Monarchy Men called for the abolition of all government 'in order to pave the way for the dominion of Christ, whose second coming was suddenly expected'. The most radical of the religious sects even proposed the ultimate absurdity of suspending the obligations of morality and natural law. For during this period, Hume commented, religion 'may be regarded as the great spring of men's actions and determinations' and 'a thick cloud of bigotry and ignorance . . . overspread the nation'.[41] Only a leader like Oliver Cromwell, who shared the republicanism and religious zealotry of the times, could have hoped to control this 'bold fanaticism' and create, a successful new political and ecclesiastical order. And in this, Hume concluded, he failed.

Hume was fascinated by Cromwell. He was the embodiment of the militant enthusiasm which had destroyed the monarchy, and was, as such, 'suited to the age in which he lived, and to that alone'. Cromwell's admirers had always venerated his austere statesmanship and his lofty sense of purpose. He alone of England's rulers had seemed to embody the spirit of republican Rome. Hume would have none of it. Cromwell was a complex and unattractive mixture of fanaticism, prejudice and political cunning, a man whose judgement was constantly clouded by delusions and who died wracked by superstition, melancholy and religious terror.

> Transported to a degree of madness with religious extasies, he never forgot the political purposes, to which they might serve. Hating monarchy, while a subject; despising liberty, while a citizen; though he retained for a time all orders of men under a seeming obedience to the parliament; he was secretly paving the way, by artifice and courage, to his own unlimited authority.[42]

But Cromwell had to be judged by the problems of the age and by his success in turning Britain into a stable republic. Hume's analysis of the Instrument of Government which established the Protectorate in 1653 showed that, so far from being a perfect system of liberty, it was more arbitrary, more despotic and – the final irony – more unstable than Charles's supposed tyranny had been. It was 'a motley piece', neither a tyranny nor a republic, which few contemporaries admired and which survived only because it was supported by the army. Cromwell's 'usurpation', Hume concluded, 'was the effect of necessity, as well as of ambition; nor is it easy to see how the various factions would at that time have been restrained, without a mixture of military and arbitrary authority'. And his regime survived only because, '[though] it was less odious to every party than that of any other party, yet it was entirely acceptable to none'.[43]

Hume, always a good historian of governments in decay, spent much time on the disintegration of the Protectorate after Cromwell's death. He wanted to show republican readers that republics were difficult to manage, particularly when their politics were saturated with religious zealotry. But he also wanted to show Whigs, Tories and Jacobites that there was nothing providential about the restoration of the Stuart monarchy in 1660 and that it had nothing whatever to do with the restoration of an ancient constitution. Charles II's restoration had taken place in the midst of the confusion – or, as he once said, 'anarchy' – which followed the death of Cromwell. Charles gained a throne and England avoided civil war because of one extraordinary accident, General Monk's defection from the parliamentary army. It was this which had enabled elections for a new parliament to be called and these had tapped popular opinion which had become as violently hostile to the enthusiasm and zealotry of the Protectorate as it had once been to the monarchy of Charles I.

> In a space of a few months, without effusion of blood, by his cautious and disinterested conduct *alone* [my italics], he had bestowed settlement on three kingdoms, which had been torne with the most violent convulsions: and having obstinately refused the most inviting conditions, offered him by the king as well as by every party in the kingdom, he freely restored his injured master to the vacant throne.[44]

For Hume Charles II came to the throne as a patriot king who rose above party and ruled with the love of his people. Initially, he seemed determined to govern within the law and 'to abolish the distinction of parties and had chosen his ministers from among all denominations'. And, for a time, the nation responded.

> In England, the civil distinctions seemed to be abolished by the leniety and equality of Charles's administration. Cavalier and Round-head were heard of no more: All men seemed to concur in submitting to the king's lawful prerogatives, and in cherishing the first privileges of the people and parliament. Theological controversy alone [he commented ominously] still subsisted, and kept alive some sparks of that flame, which had thrown the nation into combustion. While catholics, independents, and other sectaries were content with entertaining some prospect of toleration; prelacy and presbytery struggled for superiority, and the hopes and fears of both parties kept them in agitation.[45]

This was to invoke a favourite eighteenth-century image: a monarchy which was already on its last legs. By the time Hume finished the *History*, George III would have ascended the throne and set in motion his own naive and clumsy attempt to abolish party and rule as a patriot king. No one who had read Hume's account of Charles's reign could fail to realize the difficulty of governing as a patriot king in a country with a mixed constitution. As Hume commented,

> In every mixed government, such as that of England, the bulk of the nation will always incline to preserve the entire frame of the constitution; but according to the various prejudices, interests and dispositions of men, some will ever attach themselves with more passion to the regal, others to the popular part of the government. [46]

Divisions between Court and country were built into the fabric of any mixed constitution and, in the case of England, these had been infused with ideology as a result of the Civil War. Royalists feared 'the friends of liberty' who sought to limit the powers of the monarchy; the Church of England feared Presbyterianism, popery and toleration; and 'indifferent and impartial persons' feared that 'zeal for liberty should engraft itself on fanaticism, and should once more kindle a civil war in the kingdom'.[47] Charles's kingship would have to be judged by his success in maintaining a regular relationship between

Crown and Parliament at a time when the Crown had none of the patronage and influence it was to enjoy in the age of Walpole. All Charles could hope to do was to avoid conflict with Parliament. In this he was conspicuously unsuccessful.

Hume was hard on Charles; he once said that if his history of the early Stuarts had been Tory, that of their successors was Whig. 'Upon the whole', he reflected, 'I wish the two Volumes had been published together. Neither one Party nor the other, wou'd, in that Case, have had the least Pretext of reproaching me with Partiality.'[48] He thought that Charles had the intelligence, tolerance and adroitness his father and grandfather had so conspicuously lacked. On the other hand, he was fatally idle and self-indulgent and lacked political seriousness. For Charles's government had the effect of wilfully eroding much of his natural support. And this had the effect of again pushing the country to the edge of civil war.

It was the imprudence of Charles's government and his failure to manage a political system which was well within his competence to understand that Hume criticized. His notorious popish sympathies, his secretive and indiscreet dealings with Louis XIV and the corrupt and sometimes arbitrary government of the Cabal, gradually created an atmosphere of uncertainty and distrust which sharpened Court and Country divisions and served as a breeding ground for new fears that the constitution and the Church were in danger. By 1677 regular party divisions had reappeared which, as Hume reminded his readers, were rather different from those of the modern age.

> The house of commons was now regularly divided into two parties, the court and the country. Some were enlisted in the court party by offices, nay, a few by bribes secretly given them; a practice first begun by Clifford, a dangerous minister: But great numbers were attached merely by inclination; so far as they esteemed the measures of the court agreeable to the interests of the nation. Private views and faction had likewise drawn several into the country party: But there were also many of that party, who had no other object than the public good. These disinterested members on both sides fluctuated between the factions: and gave the superiority sometimes to the court, sometimes to the opposition.[49]

That was ominous enough; worse was to follow. Rumour and uncertainty, those fateful Humean solvents of habit and loyalty, had raised fears of arbitrary government and popery as well as of misgovernment. And, as the history of the early Stuart reigns had shown, in the right circumstances that toxic mixture of liberty and enthusiasm was capable of wreaking political havoc. This was the context in which Hume set his account of the Popish Plot of 1678, that extraordinary fabrication in which it was claimed that the Jesuits proposed to unseat the King and replace him with his Catholic brother. Once again religious enthusiasm threatened to subvert a fragile constitution. The Commons became 'furious' as well as factious and incapable of understanding their own or the country's own best interests. Indeed, they seemed perfectly capable of precipitating a new civil war.

Hume's discussion of the mass hysteria that gave birth to the plot is succinct, subtle and memorable and gives one a foretaste of the greatest of all such descriptions, Sir Walter Scott's account of the Porteous Riots in *The Heart of Midlothian*.

> Some mysterious design was still suspected in every enterprize and profession: Arbitrary power and popery were apprehended as the scope of all projects: Each breath or rumour made the people start with anxiety: Their enemies, they thought, were in their very bosom, and had gotten possession of their sovereign's confidence. While in this timorous, jealous disposition, the cry of a *plot* all on a sudden struck their ears: They were wakened from their slumber; and like men affrighted and in the dark, took every figure for a spectre. The terror of each man became the source of terror to another. And an universal panic being diffused, reason and argument and common sense and common humanity lost all influence over them. From this disposition of men's minds we are to account for the progress of the POPISH PLOT, and the credit given to it; an event, which would otherwise appear prodigious and altogether inexplicable.[50]

As always what mattered were the political consequences of religious enthusiasm: these were found in the Exclusion Crisis of 1679–81, the attempt to exclude the Duke of York from the succession. The 'violent hurricane' of anti-popery had fuelled politics with new ideological disagreements about the nature of monarchy in a mixed constitution, setting party politics on a new and bitterly adversarial path.

> For . . . this year [1680] is remarkable for being the epoch of the well-known epithets of WHIG and TORY, by which, and sometimes without any material difference, this island has been so long divided. The court party reproached their antagonists with their affinity to the fanatical conventiclers in Scotland, who were known by the name of whigs: The country party found a resemblance between the courtiers and the popish banditti in Ireland, to whom the appellation of tory was affixed. And after this manner, these foolish terms of reproach came into public and general use; and even at present seem not nearer their end than when they were first invented.[51]

As so often, Hume was at his most acute when discussing the effects of religion on political understanding, and his account of Whig myopia is trenchant. It was not unreasonable to call for the exclusion of a Catholic from the throne of a violently anti-Catholic country. But anti-popery had blinded them to the consequences of interfering with hereditary succession and opening the door to elective monarchy, a problem which Charles, like Hume, understood very well.

> A method was there chalked out, by which the nation, on every new reign, could be ensured of having a parliament, which the king should not, for a certain time, have it in his power to dissolve. In the case of a popish successor, the prince was to forfeit the right of conferring any ecclesiastical preferrments: No member of the privy council, no judge of the common law or in chancery, was to be put in or displaced but by consent of parliament: And the same precaution was extended to the military part of the government.[52]

This was an ingenious proposal 'of the utmost importance, [depriving] the successor of the chief branches of royalty' and strengthening the powers of Parliament. At the same time, it removed the dangers to hereditary monarchy which were inherent in the Exclusion Bill. It ought to have satisfied the interests of all parties and yet it satisfied none.

Hume's contempt for claims that Parliament had been a watchdog of liberty during Charles's reign redoubled when he turned to the short reign of his brother James II, from 1685 to 1688, and when he reflected on the Glorious Revolution. He agreed that James intended to create arbitrary government in Britain. He ruled without ministers. He continued to undermine the liberties of the boroughs. He tyrannized Scotland and Ireland. His government was often violent and cruel, and 'nobody could then doubt but that the king intended to rule by fear rather than love'.[53] He attempted to undermine the Church by establishing toleration as a prelude to popery. And he had done all of this with the help of Parliament. He even claimed dispensing powers from Parliament which would have allowed him to override the law and invade the Church and constitution whenever he pleased. And while Parliament protested against the dispensing power, it 'conferred an additional revenue on the Crown; and by rendering the king in some degree independent, contributed to increase those dangers, with which they had so much reason to be alarmed'.[54] Indeed,

> While every motive, civil and religious, concurred to alienate from the king every rank and denomination of men, it might be expected, that his throne would, without delay, fall to pieces by its own weight: But such is the influence of established government; so averse are men from beginning hazardous enterprizes; that, had not an attack been made from abroad, affairs might long have remained in their present delicate situation, and James might at last have prevailed in his rash, and ill concerted projects.[55]

What prevented that catastrophe was the King's sudden and unexpected and fateful decision to flee the country, and this, Hume thought, could be attributed largely to William of Orange. For William appears in Hume's narrative as a prudent, self-interested monarch, who was anxious to use Britain's military resources in his campaigns against Louis XIV. It was William's skill and resolution in stepping up the military and political pressure on the King to give up his throne that encouraged James to take flight. 'Men beheld all of a sudden, the reins of government thrown up by the hand which held them; and saw none, who had any right or even pretension, to take possession of them.'[56] Government had indeed been dissolved as Whigs and republicans had always argued. But while the people had become 'masters' they were in no position to draft a new contract of government as Whigs so fondly believed. Indeed there was now 'no disorder, which during their present ferment, might not be dreaded from them'. Bloodshed had been avoided simply because William's skill had ensured that a Convention Parliament had been summoned with the minimum of fuss and the people had submitted to his government 'as if he had succeeded in the most regular manner to the vacant throne'.[57] To whom, then, did modern Britons owe the Whig constitution? Certainly not to the wisdom of the Convention Parliament, which quickly degenerated into faction as it debated the terms on which William should be offered the throne. 'Never surely was national debate more important, or managed by more able speakers,' Hume commented. 'Yet is one surprised to find the topics, insisted on by both sides, so frivolous; more resembling the verbal disputes of the schools than the solid reasonings of statesmen and legislators.'[58] Once again, faction and ideology threatened political stability. And Hume ended the *History* by showing that it was William, not Parliament, who played the decisive part in settling the shape of the Revolution monarchy. He attended the acrimonious theoretical debates about the principles on which the new monarchy should be founded; whether he or his Stuart wife should be regarded as sovereign, or whether he should be regarded as regent for a future Protestant prince of the Stuart line. He listened to them in total silence,

> as if he had been no wise concerned in these transactions. And so far from forming cabals with the leaders of parties, he disdained even to bestow caresses on those whose assistance might be useful to him. This conduct was highly meritorious, and discovered great moderation and magnanimity.

He told the leaders of Parliament 'that it belonged to the parliament, now chosen and assembled with freedom, to concert measures for the public settlement; and he pretended not to interpose in their determinations'.

> He heard of several schemes proposed for establishing the government: Some insisted on a regent; others were desirous of bestowing the crown

on [his wife] the princess: It was their concern alone to chuse the plan
of administration most agreeable or advantageous to them . . . If they
judged it proper to settle a regent, he had no objection: He only thought
it incumbent on him to inform them, that he was determined not to be
the regent, nor ever to engage in a scheme, which, he knew, would be
exposed to such insuperable difficulties . . . His affairs abroad were too
important to be abandoned for so precarious a dignity, or even to allow
him so much leisure as would be requisite to introduce order into their
disjointed government.[59]

It was this threat that put an end to the debate and forced Parliament
to offer William the throne. The political prudence of a self-
interested usurper, not the wisdom of Parliament, had saved Britain
from a new civil war. As a result, Britain was to acquire a mixed constitution in which the powers of the monarchy were defined more
precisely, and a quarrelsome party system was more firmly embedded, than ever before. It was, Hume concluded, 'if not the best
system of government, at least the most entire system of liberty,
that ever was known amongst mankind'.[60]

The history of the later Stuarts lacks the intellectual pace and excitement of the first volume, and Hume himself thought it far less good:
'the Subject [of the first] was more noble, and admitted both of greater
Ornaments of Eloquence, and nicer Distinctions of Reasoning'.[61] But
it is interestingly organized for all that. It looks back to the disastrous
history of the Interregnum, in which politics had been overwhelmed
by religious enthusiasm, and forward to the age of Walpole, in which
patronage and politeness offered the first opportunity of removing the
inconveniences of the mixed constitution. Thus the Restoration monarchy had been a transitional monarchy, vulnerable to faction which
the Court had no means of controlling and to the religious enthusiasm which it had inherited from the Civil War. On the other hand, not
even the enthusiasm released by the Popish Plot had been able to
destroy the constitution. It had been absorbed into party politics, and
Hume was struck by the fact that countrymen and Whigs had begun
to call themselves the 'good and honest party' rather than describing

themselves as the 'godly party', as they had done during the Civil War, 'a sure prognostic, that their measures were not to be so furious, nor their pretensions so exorbitant'.[62] But the Crown still lacked the influence it was to enjoy in the age of Walpole. It had been impossible to regularize its relations with Parliament, and politics stayed subject to the fluctuations of speculative opinions in Parliament. But even here, Hume thought, there was room for cautious optimism. Taste was changing; there was a greater respect for order, precision and regularity in the arts and sciences as well as in matters of law and government, and this was something which could combat superstition and enthusiasm, contain faction and give men and women better ideas of their interests. In other words, there were signs that the fluctuations of opinion which had unsettled the political world of the early Stuarts were becoming more firmly anchored in ideas of interest and order. It was something that had prevented politics collapsing into civil war in the years before the Glorious Revolution and had the power to do so again in the age of Walpole. Hume's conclusion was that of a Whig who believed in modernity and lived in the hope that true liberty – the liberty which could be enjoyed only in a stable polity – had at last become possible in the modern era. But it was the conclusion of a Whig committed to philosophy and politeness who continued to fear for the future of the constitution.

6

The History of England: 2
The Tudors and the Early History of England

With the publication of the second Stuart volume, Hume's plans for a history had reached a watershed. He now had to decide whether to go forward to 1714 and the end of the Stuart era or back to the Tudors and the origins of the constitution the early Stuarts had inherited. Going forward would mean venturing into highly sensitive political territory. Going back was problematical because it involved the period before the Union of the Crowns and the creation of a British monarchy. Hume explained the dilemma to his friend William Mure in February 1757:

> I am a little uncertain what Work I shall next undertake: For I do not care to be long idle. I think you seem to approve of my going forward, and I am sensible, that the Subject is much more interesting to us, & even will be so [to] Posterity than any other I coud chuse: But can I hope, that there are Materials for composing a just & sure History of it? I am afraid not. However I shall examine the Matter. I fancy it will be requisite for me to take a Journey to London, and settle there for some time, in order to gather such Materials as are not to be found in Print. But if I should go backwards, and write the History of England from the Accession of Henry the 7th, I might remain where I am; and I own to you, at my time of Life, these Changes of Habitation are not agreeable, even tho the Place be better to which one removes.[1]

In fact the decision to go back was all but made and Hume told his publisher in May 1757 that the first of the two Tudor volumes was already 'a little advanced'. Starting with Henry VII was the right thing to do. 'It is properly at that Period modern History commences. America was discovered: Commerce extended: the Arts cultivated: Printing invented: Religion reform'd: And all the Governments of Europe almost chang'd. I wish therefore I had begun here at first.'[2] The history was published in two volumes in 1759 under the title *The History of England. Under the House of Tudor.* The project for completing the History of Great Britain under the House of Stuart was put on hold and would eventually be abandoned.

Reading the *History of England* as Hume wrote it, moving backwards in time from the Stuart to the Tudor era and from thence to what he always regarded as the prehistory of modern Britain, it is possible to detect a subtle change of mood in Hume's historical thinking. His perspective on the Stuart era was that of a historian of Walpolian Britain. The history of the Tudors, however, was the work of a Stuart historian whose sense of historical perspective was set by his discoveries about the Stuart constitution. In the same way, his account of English prehistory, from the Roman invasion to the accession of the first Tudor king, Henry VII, in 1485, reads as the work of a Tudor historian who wanted to define the relationship between the absolute and arbitrary government of Tudor England and the baronial system that flourished and decayed in the feudal era. If Hume was, as he always claimed to be, a sceptical Whig, his Whiggery encouraged him to view civilizations in the light of those which displaced them. On the other hand, as a sceptic, he was always mindful that the fortunes of any age were peculiar to itself and to that age alone. Modern Whigs like Hervey and Defoe had encouraged their contemporaries to turn their backs on a past which was distasteful and irrelevant to the present. But Hume had much better reason than they to understand the hold the past had on modern minds. His own particular contribution to modern Whiggery was to show his readers how to distance themselves from a past they could not ignore and could only hope to understand. It is this spirit above all that animates his account of the history of the Tudors, the history of the feudal era and the *longue durée* of English history.

Like Rapin, Hume realized that the key to understanding the history of the early Stuart era lay in the Elizabethan constitution, and his treatment of Elizabeth was, in some ways, the most ambitious part of the whole history. Not only was she the only monarch to whom he gave an entire volume, but the first of the Tudor volumes was more purely contextual than any other, and was designed to explore the foundations of the system of government that the Queen had perfected. Both volumes revolved around Hume's remarkable account of the Reformation, 'one of the greatest events in history', which had had the most profound influence on the making of the modern British polity.[3] It was a subject which had been treated gingerly or polemically by historians. Hume's remarkable and historic achievement was to show how it should be treated by a secular historian. In the process he was to extend and deepen the range of political history and launch a new onslaught on Christianity.

Like the rest of his history, the *History of the Tudors* was not for those in search of new data, and much of the swiftly moving narrative was distilled from Rapin's and Carte's massive tomes. His story was that of a modern Whig who thought that Henry VII and his successors had created a system of arbitrary, absolute monarchy which Elizabeth had perfected and bequeathed to the unfortunate Stuarts. His problem was to set that story in the context of the decay of feudalism and the progress of the Reformation. Hume was to discuss the decay of the feudal system in the last volume of the history; here he only had time to indicate its effects. As he said of the declining fashion for maintaining large, armed, feudal retinues,

> The encrease of the arts, more effectually than all the severities of law, put an end to this pernicious practice. The nobility, instead of vying with each other, in the number and boldness of their retainers, acquired by degrees a more civilized species of emulation, and endeavoured to excel in the splendour and elegance of their equipage, houses, and tables. The common people, no longer maintained in vicious idleness by their superiors, were obliged to learn some calling or industry, and became useful both to themselves and to others. And it must be acknowledged, in spite of those who declaim so violently against refinement in the arts, or what they are pleased to call luxury, that, as much as an industrious tradesman is both a better man and a better citizen than one of those idle retainers, who formerly depended on the great

families; so much is the life of a modern nobleman more laudable than that of an ancient baron.[4]

The political consequences of this story provided the backdrop to the history of the Tudors. It explained the decline of baronial feuding, the rise of the Commons and, above all, the sudden and spectacular transformation of a feudal monarchy which had been at the mercy of the baronage into the absolute and arbitrary monarchy which modern Whigs like Hume thought the Tudors had created. Hume presented Henry VII as a feudal warlord who had won his kingship in battle and came to the throne bringing with him 'all the partialities which belong to the head of a faction'. In his hands the law had simply been a convenient weapon for breaking his enemies and lining his own pocket – for avarice, Hume thought, was his 'ruling passion'.[5] His rule was arbitrary, irregular and often oppressive, and rested on the grudging consent of a weakened baronage which thought him 'so much the less burthensome, as by his extending royal authority, and curbing the rebels he became in reality the sole oppressor in his kingdom'.[6] No doubt he had ruled with the consent of Parliament and derived much of his enormous authority from statute. On the other hand, throughout the Tudor era, Parliament always proved to be a willing and servile ally of arbitrary and even tyrannical government. The gentry might have been emancipated from the nobility. On the other hand, their minds were still servile. As the history of the early Tudor parliaments showed, their chief characteristic was parsimony in matters of taxation and abject servility in aiding and abetting the growth of arbitrary government. As ever, it was important to remember that changes in opinion could not always be deduced from changes in property. Indeed, so far from marking a return to constitutional government, Henry's reign saw the final destruction of an ancient constitution that had existed in some form or other since Saxon times and had been one of the principal casualties of the confusions of the civil wars of the later Middle Ages. It was yet another demonstration of the principle that 'the English constitution, like all others, has been in a state of continual fluctuation'.[7]

If Henry VII had finally destroyed the ancient constitution of England, his son Henry VIII destroyed its ancient religion, uniting Church and state under his sole jurisdiction, immeasurably extending his power and laying the foundations of what ought to have become a cohesive absolute monarchy. Hume saw Henry VIII as the first modern king of England, a prince with a taste for war, diplomacy, culture and luxury which stood in striking contrast to the narrow gothic tastes of his father and was fortified, Hume noticed shrewdly, by that taste for theology which was characteristic of Renaissance princes. Henry came to the throne at a time of fundamental change in the European state system. It was a period in which the kings of France and Spain were extending and consolidating their kingdoms and redrawing the diplomatic map of Europe, 'hastening fast to the situation, in which they have remained, without any material alteration, for near three centuries'.[8] Abroad, Henry established himself as an imperial prince. At home, he left civil and ecclesiastical government in the hands of Cardinal Wolsey, who ruled the Church 'as if he himself were pope', extending and regularizing civil government 'by a strict administration of Justice . . . and no Chancellor ever discovered greater impartiality in his decisions, deeper penetration of judgement, or more enlarged knowledge of law and equity'.[9] Indeed, Henry and Wolsey between them seemed unwittingly to be laying the foundations of that most desirable Humean form of government, a civilized absolute monarchy. It was a development which would be profoundly interrupted by the Reformation.

Hume saw Henry's unsuccessful campaign to divorce an unsatisfactory wife, the break between the English and the Roman Church and the establishment of the Church of England under his own governance in 1534 as the outcome of a crisis in international relations. He thought that Henry had an unanswerable case for a divorce. He also thought it significant that the prospect of a Church under the governance of a prince was just as agreeable to the King's 'ecclesiastical subjects' as it was to the laity.

> The acknowledgement of the king's supremacy introduced there a greater simplicity in the government, by uniting the spiritual with the civil power, and preventing disputes about limits, which never could be exactly determined between the contending jurisdictions. A way was also prepared for checking the exorbitancies of superstition, and break-

ing those shackles, by which all human reason, policy, and industry had so long been encumbered. The prince, it may be supposed, being head of the religion, as well as of the temporal jurisdiction of the kingdom, though he might sometimes employ the former as an engine of government, had no interest, like the Roman pontiff, in nourishing its excessive growth; and, except when blinded by his own ignorance or bigotry, would be sure to retain it within tolerable limits, and prevent its abuses. And on the whole, there followed from this revolution many beneficial consequences; though perhaps neither forseen nor intended by the persons who had the chief hand in conducting it.[10]

But the great test of Henry's statesmanship was to be his success in weathering the theological storms which were let loose by the Reformation. Here what mattered was the confusion of sectarian tongues and the priestcraft which turned words into weapons and diverted men's minds from the ordinary business of life to the often furious pursuit of ghostly visions of eternal happiness or damnation. Reducing the history of religion to the history of priestcraft was, of course, a way of attacking religion itself. The deceptively short and simple 'digression' on priestcraft marked a new stage in Hume's assault on Christianity and represented the first serious attempt to write a civil history of religion in Britain. As such it is well worth quoting in full.

Why, Hume asked, must there be 'an ecclesiastical order, and a public establishment of religion in every civilized community?' He answered,

> Most of the arts and professions in a state are of such a nature, that, while they promote the interest of the society, they are also useful or agreeable to some individuals; and in that case, the constant rule of the magistrate, except, perhaps, on the first introduction of any art, is, to leave the profession to itself, and trust its encouragement to those who reap the benefit of it. The artizans, finding their profits to rise by the favour of their customers, encrease, as much as possible, their skill and industry; and as matters are not disturbed by any injudicious tampering, the commodity is always sure to be at all times nearly proportioned to the demand.
>
> But there are also some callings, which, though useful and even nec-

essary in a state, bring no particular advantage or pleasure to any individual; and the supreme power is obliged to alter its conduct with regard to the retainers of those professions. It must give them public encouragement in order to their subsistence [*sic*]; and it must provide against that negligence, to which they will naturally be subject, either by annexing peculiar honours to the profession, by establishing a long subordination of ranks and a strict dependance, or by some other expedient. The persons, employed in the finances, armies, fleets, and magistracy, are instances of this order of men.

It may naturally be thought, at first sight, that the ecclesiastics belong to the first class, and that their encouragement, as well as that of lawyers and physicians, may safely be entrusted to the liberality of individuals, who are attached to their doctrines, and who find benefit or consolation from their spiritual ministry and assistance. Their industry and vigilance will, no doubt, be whetted by such an additional motive; and their skill in the profession, as well as their address in governing the minds of the people, must receive daily encrease, from their increasing practice, study, and attention.

But if we consider the matter more closely, we shall find, that this interested diligence of the clergy is what every wise legislator will study to prevent; because in every religion, except the true, it is highly pernicious, and it has even a natural tendency to pervert the true, by infusing into it a strong mixture of superstition, folly, and delusion. Each ghostly practitioner, in order to render himself more precious and sacred in the eyes of his retainers, will inspire them with the most violent abhorrence of all other sects, and continually endeavour, by some novelty, to excite the languid devotion of his audience. No regard will be paid to truth, morals, or decency in the doctrines inculcated. Every tenet will be adopted that best suits the disorderly affections of the human frame. Customers will be drawn to each conventicle by new industry and address in practising on the passions and credulity of the populace. And in the end, the civil magistrate will find, that he has dearly paid for his pretended frugality, in saving a fixed establishement for the priests; and that in reality the most decent and advantageous composition, which he can make with the spiritual guides, is to bribe their indolence, by assigning stated salaries to their profession, and rendering it superfluous for them to be farther active, than merely to prevent their flock from straying in quest of new pastures. And in this manner ecclesiastical establishments, though commonly they arose at first from religious views, prove in the end advantageous to the political interests of society.[11]

Here was the historian of commerce reducing the history of religion to a relationship between the clergy and their 'customers'. But here also was a story of the clergy as quacks, trading on the ignorance and superstition of rich and poor, extending their power and profit, jeopardizing the security of their customers' earthly property and happiness for the sake of eternal happiness. By Luther's day, Hume observed, the Roman Catholic clergy had acquired 'large revenues, privileges, immunities, and powers', making them politically formidable, sometimes cynical about the doctrines on which their power rested. It took Martin Luther, 'an Austin friar' who had been educated in the same strict theological principles as Hume, to rouse mankind from its lethargy and question the authority of the Church. 'The quick and surprising progress' of his ideas could be explained by the spread of scholarship and printing, and 'the minds of men, somewhat awakened from a profound sleep of so many centuries, were prepared for every novelty, and scrupled less to tread in any unusual path which was opened to them'. The stage was set for a revolution in opinion in a society which was already changing. The Catholic Church's authority was enshrined in the central dogma of the Real Presence, that miraculous transformation of bread and wine into the body and blood of Christ, and it was reinforced by auricular confession and the power of priests to grant the remission of sins. Both of these doctrines, Hume pointed out, had the natural tendency to increase the power of the clergy and the subjection of the people. These were the dogmas that the Protestants had attempted to undermine. 'In contradiction to the multiplied superstitions, with which [the Roman Church] was loaded, [the Lutherans] adopted an enthusiastic strain of devotion, which admitted no observances, rites or ceremonies, but placed all merit in a mysterious species of faith, in inward vision, rapture and ecstasy'.[12] Private judgement was challenging priestly authority and, under these circumstances, it was inevitable that sects which thrived on questioning secular as well as religious authority would abound.

Hume thought that Henry's response to this problem was effective but absurd. His 'rough hand' was well adapted for dissolving the monasteries, 'rendering asunder those bands by which the ancient superstition had fastened itself on the kingdom', and for establishing his dominion over the new Church.[13] But his solution to the doctrinal question could be explained only in terms of the superstitions, prejudices and passions of a tyrant. The Six Articles of 1539, which spelled out the articles of faith of the Henrican Church, simply re-established the old doctrine of the Real Presence, 'that very doctrine, in which among the numberless victories of superstition over common sense, her triumph is the most signal and egregious'. On the other hand, as Hume pointed out, it was formulated in such a way that both Catholics and Protestants found it profoundly objectionable and it had to be imposed on both parties with the utmost tuthlessness, establishing 'the uniformity in opinion, on which he was so intent'. In making his superstitions 'a rule for the nation' he avoided the fatal trap of allowing the new Church to fall into the hands of a religious party.[14] What is more, all this was done with the help of a parliament whose 'submissive, not to say slavish disposition . . . made it the more easy for him to assume and maintain that entire dominion, by which his reign is so much distinguished in the English history'. Indeed, Hume concluded with relish, by this time the English were so thoroughly subdued 'that like eastern slaves, they were inclined to admire those acts of violence and tyranny, which were exercised over themselves, and at their own expence'.[15]

Although Hume made few bones about Henry's bigotry and cruelty in imposing uniformity on his Church he seemed willing to condone it, merely commenting that while Henry's absolute, uncontrouled authority' entitled him to the appellation of a great prince, 'his tyranny and barbarity exclude him from the character of a good one'.[16] For Henry's ruthless hand had at least prevented England from sliding into the horrors of religious civil war, which had begun to devastate Europe and threatened England after his death. Under his Protestant son Edward VI, who reigned from 1547 to 1553, and Edward's Catholic sister Mary, who reigned from 1553 to 1558, 'the hopes of the Protestants and the fears of the Catholics began to revive and the zeal of these parties produced every where disputes and animosities, the usual preludes to more fatal divisions'.[17] All of this was to be evident to Elizabeth, who came to the throne in 1558 having already been exposed to the zealotry and faction of her brother's and her sister's short reigns. She had seen the consequences of the violent religious oscillations which had first of all turned England into a Protestant and then into a Catholic state. She had seen the cruelty and imprudence of punishing heresies by fire, 'a very natural method of reconciling the Kingdom to the Romish communion', Hume commented sourly.[18]

On her accession, Elizabeth had set about cultivating politicians and clerics of all but the most objectionable persuasions – always a welcome sign to Hume that a monarch was above party and faction. She made her peace abroad. 'She immediately recalled the [Protestant] exiles, and gave liberty to prisoners, who were confined on account of religion.' At the same time she took care to stamp out anti-popish preaching.

> Open in her address, gracious and affable in all public appearances, she rejoiced in the concourse of her subjects, entered into all their pleasures and amusements, and without departing from her dignity, which she knew well how to preserve, she acquired a popularity beyond what any of her predecessors or successors ever could attain. Her own sex exulted to see a woman hold the reins of empire with such prudence and fortitude: And while a young princess of twenty-five years (for that was her age at her accession) who possessed all the graces and insinuation, though not all the beauty of her sex, courted the affection of individuals by her civilities, of the public by her services, her authority, though corroborated by the strictest bands of law and religion, appeared to be derived entirely from the choice and inclination of the people.[19]

But the ultimate test of Elizabeth's prudence lay in her religious settlement. Hume went out of his way to show that the dogmas, disciplines and institutions of the Elizabethan Church, like Henry's, were entirely of her own making and were the work of a queen who was determined not to let the Church become a prey to party. It was a remarkable piece of work. 'In one session, without violence, tumult or clamour, was the whole system of religion altered, on the very commencement of a reign, and by the will of a young woman, whose title to the crown was by many thought liable to great objections.'[20] Hume saw the monarchy that Elizabeth created in the first year of her reign as the apogee of Tudor government. It was a system of arbitrary government built on foundations laid by her father and grandfather out of the rubble of a decayed feudal system and a corrupt Catholic Church. It united civil and ecclesiastical power in the hands of a sovereign who was to devote the rest of her long reign to jealously safeguarding her authority. It was a monarchy born of arbitrary power and depending on it for its survival. The rest of his long account of Elizabeth's reign was a philosophical historian's account of what modern Whigs had thought of as a 'tyranny'.

Once again, Hume chose a striking context for the history of Elizabeth's governance: the religious wars of contemporary Europe. As he pointed out, the peculiar problem of her age was the religious turmoil from which no European state was immune. Great and civilized monarchies like France and Spain, like poor and barbarous countries like Scotland, were torn apart by religious divisions. In France, personal rivalries erupted into religious dissensions:

> Condé, Coligni, Andelot, assembled their friends, and flew to arms: Guise and Montmorency got possession of the king's person, and constrained the queen-regent to embrace their party: Fourteen armies were levied and put in motion in different parts of France: each province, each city, each family, was agitated with intestine rage and animosity. The father was divided against the son; brother against brother; and women themselves, sacrificing their humanity as well as their timidity to the religious fury, distinguished themselves by acts of ferocity and valour. Wherever the hugonots prevailed, the images were broken, the altars pillaged, the churches demolished, the monasteries consumed with fire: Where success attended the catholics, they burned the bibles, re-baptized the infants, constrained married persons to pass anew through the nuptial ceremony: And plunder, desolation, and bloodshed attended equally the triumph of both parties. The parliament of Paris itself, the seat of law and justice, instead of employing its authority to compose these fatal quarrels, published an edict, by which it put the sword into the hands of the enraged multitude, and empowered the

catholics everywhere to massacre the hugonots: And it was during this period, when men began to be somewhat enlightened, and in this nation, renowned for polished manners, that the theological rage, which had long been boiling in men's veins, seems to have attained its last stage of virulence and ferocity.[21]

England had avoided such turmoil 'partly from the interposition of the civil magistrate in this innovation, partly to the gradual and slow steps, by which the reformation was conducted in [England]'.[22] Scotland was not so lucky. Here was an ambitious and factious baronage beyond the control of even a skilful ruler like Mary of Guise, who had governed Scotland as regent from 1554 to 1559. Here was an overbearing Catholic Church and here too were correspondingly zealous Presbyterian reformers dominated by that fearsome and overbearing 'rustic apostle' John Knox.[23] Here extreme zealotry was combined with poverty and barbarism, providing a striking contrast to the progress of the Reformation in France as well as in England. What made it all the more interesting was that the feckless and unfortunate Mary Queen of Scots, who succeeded to the throne as an infant in 1542 and ruled until her enforced abdication in 1567, possessed a claim to the English throne which was all the more menacing to Elizabeth by virtue of the fact that she was a Catholic.

All of this provided Hume with a point of entry to that classic *cause célèbre* of popular eighteenth-century historiography, the Marian Controversy. By Hume's time, the sufferings of a hapless Catholic queen who had been deposed by Presbyterian zealots and executed by an envious and tyrannical Tudor despot were being lovingly celebrated by Jacobites and Episcopalians, Scottish patriots and sentimental ladies, in the face of the startlingly polemical opposition of those who thought Mary had been an enemy to the Church, the English Crown and morality. As one of Hume's friends remarked, the issue struck up 'more zeal and bile than any question of however much greater importance that I know'.[24] Hume had a limited but healthy appetite for historical tittle-tattle and, like everyone else, had raked over the intriguing and seamy details of Mary's amours. He once startled an aged Jacobite friend, dozing in the Advocates' Library, by bellowing in his ear, 'Queen Mary was a strumpet and a murtherer.'[25] But what made her reign interesting was not her guilt or innocence of murdering husbands but her lack of prudence in dealing with her unenviable situation in Scotland and with Elizabeth. On the first count, Hume had no reservations in portraying Mary as a ruler who was out of her depth in a turbulent and dangerous kingdom and whose deposition in 1567 was hardly unexpected. And she was imprudent if not criminal as Elizabeth's prisoner in her dealings with her Catholic supporters. 'An enumeration of her qualities', Hume concluded, 'might carry the appearance of a panegyric; an account of her conduct must, in some parts, wear the aspect of severe satire and invective.'[26]

But Marians who got cold comfort from Hume's treatment of their heroine could console themselves with his treatment of Elizabeth. He insisted that she alone and not her ministers and parliaments was responsible for Mary's trial and execution. She had waited a long time 'for executing vengeance on a competitor, whom from the beginning of her reign, she had ever equally dreaded and hated'. She had found a suitable pretext in the somewhat dubious evidence of Mary's complicity in the Babington Plot, which was supposed to herald a French invasion, Elizabeth's assassination and Mary's accession to the English throne. And what was lacking in the evidence was made good by the conveniently flimsy rules of evidence required by English treason law. What mattered to Hume was that at all times Elizabeth's ministers and parliaments were entirely at her beck and call. As for her vacillation in signing Mary's death warrant, this was simply evidence of the political skill of an 'excellent hypocrite' who understood all too well what political problems the execution would cause and refused to carry out the sentence until they had been contained.[27] As for her celebrated 'loud wailings and lamentations' and her much publicized fits of fury on learning that the sentence had been carried out, these were simply an exercise in distancing herself from an action that threatened to rupture her relations with Mary's son and her own heir, James VI. For she hoped 'that she might thereby afford James a decent pretence for renewing his amity with her, on which their mutual interests so much depended'.[28] In fact, Hume's treatment of the Marian controversy was a study of Elizabethan political prudence and a demonstration of the peculiar and distinctive principles of a system of monarchy that belonged to a bygone age. The Queen's political skills were not for the squeamish and had not been understood by historians like Rapin; nor could they be expected to appeal to Hume's more sentimental readers. No doubt Elizabeth's reign had been glorious, but those glories had nothing to do with constitutionality and a respect for liberties enshrined in a supposedly ancient constitution. They consisted in preserving her kingdom from wars of religion and controlling the zealotry that caused them.

Throughout his history of Elizabeth's reign, Hume went out of his way to insist that it was prudent government on the part of an absolute and arbitrary monarch, not providence, that had preserved England from religious wars, and he never let slip an opportunity of demonstrating how quickly and decisively the Queen stamped on any threat to her authority. In matters of religion, 'of which Elizabeth was, if possible, still more jealous than of matters of state', she was constantly alert to the activities of Protestant reformers 'who indulged themselves in the most violent contrariety and antipathy to all former practices' and regarded the surplices, tippets and corner-caps worn by the Elizabethan clergy as 'a symbolizing with Antichrist'.[29] But Elizabeth was personally and politically attracted to 'mitigated superstition' in matters of religion. She distrusted attempts to shake off 'those forms and observances, which, without distracting men of more refined apprehensions, tend, in a very innocent manner, to allure, and amuse, and engage the vulgar' and, like her father, she made sure that uniformity was strictly enforced.[30] This, rather than the system of arbitrary government which James so conspicuously failed to understand, was the poisoned chalice Elizabeth left to her successor, for 'while the sovereign authority checked these excesses, the flame was confined, not extinguished; and burning fiercer from confinement, it burst out in the succeeding reigns to the destruction of the church and monarchy'.[31]

Like Thomas Carte, Hume continually reminded his readers that reformed religion had political implications which were particularly sharp in a monarchy in which the sovereign was head of Church and state.

All enthusiasts, indulging themselves in rapturous flights, extasies, visions, inspirations, have a natural aversion to episcopal authority, to ceremonies, rites, and forms, which they denominate superstition, or beggarly elements, and which seem to restrain the liberal effusions of their zeal and devotion: But there was another set of opinions adopted by these innovators, which rendered them in a peculiar manner the object of Elizabeth's aversion. The same bold and daring spirit, which accompanied them in their addresses to the divinity, appeared in their political speculations; and the principles of civil liberty, which, during some reigns, had been little avowed in the nation, and which were totally incompatible with the present exorbitant prerogative, had been strongly adopted by this new sect. Scarcely any sovereign before Elizabeth, and none after her, carried higher, both in speculation and practice, the authority of the crown; and the puritans (so these sectaries were called, on account of their pretending to a superior purity of worship and discipline) could not recommend themselves worse to her favour, than by inculcating the doctrine of resisting or restraining princes. From all these motives, the queen neglected no opportunity of depressing those zealous innovators; and while they were secretly countenanced by some of her most favoured ministers . . . she never was, to the end of her life, reconciled to their principles and practices.[32]

Puritanism was a potentially revolutionary doctrine, and it was prudent of the Queen, living in the dangerous world of sixteenth-century politics, to treat it as such. Time and again, Hume pointed out, the Queen spelled out her views on the duties and powers of Parliament in public.

They were not to canvass any matters of state: Still less were they to meddle with the church. Questions of either kind were far above their reach, and were appropriated to the prince alone, or to those councils and ministers, with whom he was pleased to entrust them. What then was the office of parliaments? They might give directions for the due tanning of leather, or milling of cloth; for the preservation of pheasants and partridges; for the reparation of bridges and highways; for the punishment of vagabonds or common beggars. Regulations concerning the police of the country came properly under their inspection; and the laws of this kind which they prescribed, had, if not a greater, yet a more durable authority, than those which were derived solely from the proclamations of the sovereign. Precedents or reports could fix a rule for decisions in private property, or the punishment of crimes; but no alteration or innovation in the municipal law could proceed from any other source than parliament; nor would the courts of justice be induced to change their established practice by an order of council. But the most acceptable part of parliamentary proceedings was the granting of subsidies; the attainting and punishing of the obnoxious nobility, or any minister of state after his fall; the countenancing of such great efforts of power, as might be deemed somewhat exceptionable, when they proceeded entirely from the sovereign. The redress of grievances was sometimes promised to the people; but seldom could have place, while it was an established rule, that the prerogatives of the crown must not be abridged, or so much as questioned and examined in parliament.[33]

As Hume emphasized, the Queen had made no secret of these views and only a handful of Puritans in Parliament ever questioned them. Indeed his most striking reply to Rapin's remarks about her sensitivity to parliamentary privilege was to point out that it was the Commons, not the Queen, which voted to imprison Peter Wentworth, the most prominent Puritan MP, for offering 'a rude sketch of those principles of liberty, which happily gained afterwards the ascendant in England', and it was the Queen, not the Commons, who pardoned him. 'By this seeming leniety', Hume commented shrewdly, 'she indirectly retained the power, which she had assumed, of imprisoning the members, and obliging them to answer before her for their conduct in Parliament.' He concluded, 'So absolute, indeed, was the authority of the crown, that the precious spark of liberty had been kindled, and was preserved, by the puritans alone, and it was to this sect, whose principles appear so frivolous and habits so ridiculous, that the English owe the whole freedom of their constitution.'[34]

In her last years, Hume commented, the Queen had become increasingly imperious and arbitrary. In the last parliament of her reign, the Commons had cautiously and justifiably criticized her practice of granting her favourites trading monopolies, 'the most intolerable for the present, and the most pernicious in their conse-quences, that ever were known in any age or under any government'. The Commons introduced a bill to abolish these monopolies; courtiers replied 'that this matter regarded the prerogative, and that the Com-mons could never hope for success', and lectured the Commons with a discourse 'more worthy of a Turkish divan than of an English House of Commons, according to our present idea of this assembly'. The Queen, 'who perceived how odious monopolies had become, and what heats were likely to arise, sent for the speaker, and desired him to acquaint the House, that she would immediately cancel the most grievous and oppressive of these patents'. To this, the Commons replied with a display of servile flattery couched in terms 'appropri-ated to the Supreme Being'. The Queen, 'by prudently receding, in time, from part of her prerogative, maintained her dignity, and pre-served the affections of her people'.[35] It was a display of prudence on the part of a monarch who understood the nature of her power exactly and was able to maintain it in a way that would be beyond the capacities of her successors.

Hume's final verdict on Elizabeth's reign is worth a moment's attention. Once again, he insisted on viewing her governance in what still remains a daring and neglected context, her success in '[preserv-ing] her people by superior prudence from the confusions in which theological controversy had converted all the neighbouring nations'. And to those who did not know what to make of the fact that she was a woman, he offered what reads like a polite sceptic's retort to John Knox's notorious *The first Blast of the Trumpet against the Mon-strous Regiment of Women*.

> When we contemplate her as a woman, we are apt to be struck with the highest admiration of her great qualities and extensive capacity; but we are also apt to require some more softness of disposition, some greater lenity of temper, some of those amiable weaknesses by which her sex is distinguished. But the true method of estimating her merit, is to lay aside all these considerations, and consider her merely as a rational being, placed in authority, and entrusted with the gov-ernment of mankind. We may find it difficult to reconcile our fancy

to her as a wife or a mistress; but her qualities as a sovereign, though with some considerable exceptions, are the object of undisputed applause and approbation.[36]

Hume's account of Elizabeth's reign is a remarkable performance. Scarcely ever does the pace of the narrative flag; scarcely ever are readers allowed to forget that their job is to exercise their judgement on the political prudence of a much revered ruler who lived in a very different age to their own. In the history of the Stuarts, the narrative had been less even, Hume's presence more irregular and intrusive, his readers being periodically hustled from one judgement to another with the help of digressions and asides. By the time he came to write about Elizabeth, his historical craftsmanship was more assured. The narrative of events proceeds on the assumption that we already know and will probably respect the rules of the Humean game and find it amusing as well as interesting. And because he was on safer party-polemical ground Hume seems to have felt more secure in devoting so much of his energy to developing the remarkable account of the Reformation which lay at the centre of his field of vision as a historian of human behaviour. For here, if anywhere, the liaison between natural and civil history was most complete; here that the grip of the Enlightenment on history most secure.

By now Hume's major task as a revisionist historian was all but done. He had identified the prehistory of the modern constitution in the rubbish of a decayed feudal system and in the world of luxury and reformation that followed. He had traced the birth of a peculiar system of monarchy which was arbitrary and irregular but rested on the consent and adulation of a servile people and parliament, who even thought of themselves as free. And, step by step, he had traced the extraordinary story of the birth of modern ideas of liberty, barely discernible in the Puritan choir which had received such rough treatment from Elizabeth but had been nurtured by the incompetence of the Stuarts. With the history of the Tudors, Hume's account of the origins of the British constitution was complete, and the umbilical cord that had hitherto tied the English historical mind to its gothic past was broken. One last historical task remained, to set the Tudor monarchy in its own historical perspective, and this was what Hume attempted in the last two volumes of the history which appeared in 1762 and dealt with *The History of England, from the Invasion of Julius Caesar to the Accession of Henry VII*.

The decision to write about 'the antient English history' was taken by the early summer of 1759 and was no doubt partly influenced by the offer of the enormous sum of £1,400 for the copyright. It was also something to do. As he told Adam Smith, 'I shall execute the Work at Leizure, without fatiguing myself by such ardent Application as I have hitherto employed. It is chiefly as a Resource against Idleness, that I shall undertake this Work: For as to Money, I have enough: And as to Reputation, what I have wrote already will be sufficient, if it be good: If not, it is not likely I shall now write better.'[37] And by giving his history a beginning, it was also and most obviously the appropriate way of providing his project with an end should he decide, as it seemed increasingly obvious he was going to resist, the temptation to complete his history of the House of Stuart.

The canvas Hume had chosen was vast in size, and the data out of which to construct a history of institutions and events more patchy and problematical than that available to historians of later periods. As a result, Hume's historical brushwork was correspondingly bolder and more schematic than hitherto and was designed to establish the contexts in which the early history of England ought to be set. For here, Hume thought, a philosophically minded historian was on surer ground.

It has become understandably fashionable to deplore the Enlightenment's inability to think of the feudal era as anything other than an unending and bloody struggle for power between kings, barons and the Church in an age which was sunk in superstition, ignorance and barbarism – a view with which modern Whigs heartily agreed. But this was anti-intellectualism directed against what Hume called the 'dark industry of antiquaries', whose scholarship had all too often been fed on the polemical desire to trace the roots of absolute or limited monarchy to the feudal era.[38] These antiquaries had, however, taken feudal society seriously, and viewed it as a form of civilization with its own regularities and political principles. Hume used his two volumes to pick bones with both views. Modern Whigs were right to think that a feudal society could not possibly support a regular form of government. On the other hand, feudal society had been regulated by its own principles, which were intelligible and worth exploring not simply because they were curious but because they showed how irrelevant the experience of the feudal age was to men and women living in an age of commerce.

In the barest of outlines, Hume's story of the millennium which spanned the Roman occupation of Britain and Henry VII's victory at Bosworth in 1485 was the work of a modern Whig. He showed how a degenerate and effeminate Saxon society had been overthrown by a ruthless army of 'Norman freebooters' in 1066, who had established a monarchy which was more powerful than any in Europe.[39] He discussed the reasons for the resurgence of baronial and ecclesiastical power during the reigns of Richard I and King John which had reached its peak in 1215 with the signing of Magna Carta. He showed how royal power had been rebuilt by 'the English Justinian' Edward I and later, after the unfortunate deposition of Edward II, by Edward III, during whose long reign England began to extend its empire in France. He wrote of England as a country in which baronial feuding and civil war became endemic after Edward's death in 1377 and in which feudalism received its *coup de grâce* from Henry VII after his victory at Bosworth in 1485. As he put it:

> The ancient history of England is nothing but a catalogue of reversals: Every thing is in fluctuation and movement: One faction is continual undoing what was established by another: And the multiplied oaths, which each party exacted for the security of the present acts, betray a perpetual consciousness of their instability.[40]

But, of course, Hume wanted to do much more than catalogue the historical prejudices of modern Whigs. He wanted to scotch, once and for all, the notion that English feudalism had been capable of supporting a regular form of government, as so many modern 'friends of liberty' thought. As he had already suggested in his *Essays* no barbarous and licentious military society like that of the Saxons could possibly have generated a system of limited monarchy which was able to maintain a regular system of government. And, even if they had, later generations would have had no reason to obey a constitution designed to service a society so different from their own.

Hume's development of this argument is fascinating. One part of his strategy was to show that England had not been lacking in able kings who would have liked to establish regular government in England. But even Alfred, the greatest of all Saxon kings, whose 'shining talents' had enabled him to defend his kingdom from 'utter ruin and subversion', who had established civil and military institutions, who had enforced the law and encouraged the spread of learning, who had rebuilt cities which had been devastated by war – even this king, 'who seems indeed to be the model of that perfect character, which, under the denomination of a sage or a wise man, philosophers have been fond of delineating, rather as a fiction of their imagination, than in hopes of ever seeing it really existing', even Alfred had been unable to establish a system of government capable of surviving his death in that barbarous Saxon age.[41] In the same way, the efforts of those remarkable Norman kings, Henry I and Henry II, to extend and regularize the power of the monarchy in the twelfth century were not enough to create a government of laws which were proof against the personal inadequacies and wickedness of Richard and King John. And not even that 'model of a politic and warlike king', Edward I, or his scarcely less accomplished grandson, Edward III, had been able to establish a system of government which could prevent the disastrous declension of a feudal society into the violence and bloodshed of the Wars of the Roses.[42] These kings had been paragons of prudence compared with the puny mortals who occupied the throne of modern England, and yet even they had failed to turn a feudal constitution into a civilized one. They had failed because English society was locked into a feudal system which had been originally designed to preserve the authority of a king in a military society. But its long-term tendency had been to undermine monarchical power and regular government and to obstruct the faltering steps the English had taken on the path to civilization. Hume's task was to explain why this had happened.

The roots of the feudal system lay in the needs of barbarous societies which were organized for war and conquest rather than

cultivation. Here, power was held by a great chieftain 'who was chosen from among the rest, on account of his superior valour or nobility;
and who derived his power from the voluntary association or attachment of the other chieftains'.

> When a tribe governed by these ideas, and actuated by these principles,
> subdued a large territory, they found, that, though it was necessary to
> keep themselves in a military posture, they could neither remain united in
> a body, nor take up their quarters in several garrisons, and that their
> manners and institutions debarred them from using these expedients; the
> obvious ones, which, in a like situation, would have been employed by a
> more civilized nation. Their ignorance in the art of finances, and perhaps
> the devastations inseparable from such violent conquests, rendered it
> impracticable for them to levy taxes sufficient for the pay of numerous
> armies; and their repugnance to the subordination, with their attachment
> to rural pleasures, made the life of the camp or garrison, if perpetuated
> during peaceful times, extremely odious and disgustful to them. They
> seized, therefore, such a portion of the conquered lands as appeared nec-
> essary; they assigned a share for supporting the dignity of their prince
> and government; they distributed other parts, under the title of fiefs, to
> the chiefs; these made a new partition among their retainers; the express
> condition of all these grants was, that they might be resumed at pleasure,
> and that the possessor, so long as he enjoyed them, should still remain in
> readiness to take the field for the defence of the nation. And though the
> conquerors immediately separated, in order to enjoy their new acquisi-
> tions, their martial disposition made them readily fulfil the terms of their
> engagement: They assembled on the first alarm; their habitual attach-
> ment to the chieftain made them willingly submit to his command; and
> thus a regular military force, though concealed, was always ready, to
> defend, on any emergence, the interest and honour of the community.[43]

In such a society, the king was only first among equals, his authority personal rather than institutional, and succession was inevitably
irregular and contentious. In such a society it was difficult for a king
to maintain rules of justice and natural for men to look to their lords
for protection. Feudal societies might look free, Hume commented,
but in reality:

the great body even of the free citizens, in those ages, really enjoyed much less true liberty, than where the execution of the laws is the most severe, and where subjects are reduced to the strictest subordination and dependance on the civil magistrate. The reason is derived from the excess itself of that liberty. Men must guard themselves at any price against insults and injuries; and where they receive not protection from the laws and magistrate, they will see it by submission to superiors, and by herding in some private confederacy, which acts under the direction of a powerful leader. And thus all anarchy is the immediate cause of tyranny, if not over the state, at least over many of the individuals.[44]

This feudal system had been introduced into England in stricter form by the Normans and had worked in favour of royal authority in the early years of the Conquest, when the conquerors had more to fear from their new subjects than from the king. The balance of interest between the Norman kings and their barons had begun to change when that threat was removed, when the barons began to regard their feudal estates as heritable property, and when they began to subdivide their estates among their own followers in return for military services to themselves. This had the inevitable consequence of increasing the power of the barons at the expense of the king and of encouraging the barons' vassals to look to their lords for protection. By the early fourteenth century, the problem was acute.

The laws had been so feebly executed, even during the long, active, and vigilant reign of Edward III, that no subject could trust to their protection. Men openly associated themselves, under the patronage of some great baron, for their mutual defence. They wore public badges, by which their confederacy was distinguished. They supported each other in all quarrels, iniquities, extortions, murders, robberies, and other crimes. Their chief was more their sovereign than the king himself; and their own band was more connected with them than their country. Hence the perpetual turbulence, disorders, factions, and civil wars of those times: Hence the small regard paid to a character or the opinion of the public: Hence the large discretionary prerogatives of the crown, and the danger which might have ensued from the too great limitation of them. If the king had possessed no arbitrary powers, while all the nobles assumed and exercised them, there must have ensued an absolute anarchy in the state.[45]

It was this built-in tendency of feudalism to limit the power of the king at the expense of the barons which made it impossible for any king to secure the rules of justice. It was why the government of Edward III, 'a prince of great capacity', was in the last resort nothing more than 'a barbarous monarchy'.[46] Limited monarchy was indeed built into the fabric of feudal society as the friends of liberty had claimed. On the other hand it was incapable of sustaining regular and civilized government.

All of this provided Hume with a setting for his discussion of the early history of Parliament, whose origins were, he thought, to be found in those baronial councils, which the Norman kings had summoned to offer advice and consent. With the decay of the feudal system these councils began to include representatives of the lesser barons and boroughs, and, later still, these were summoned to a separate chamber. But their function was not to legislate, let alone to check the authority of the king, as so many fondly believed. Like the greater barons, they were there to offer advice and consent and, so far from checking the king's power, they 'were naturally inclined to adhere to him, as the great fountain of law and justice, and to support him against the power of the aristocracy, which was at once the source of oppression to themselves, and disturbed him in the execution of the laws'.[47] The Commons of the feudal era had understood better than their modern counterparts that true liberty consisted in supporting the authority of the monarchy, not undermining it.

There is a final irony in this account of early English history which is too good to miss. Throughout, Hume had paid close attention to the role of the Church in shaping English politics and society. The Roman Church had celebrated the conversion of the first English king from paganism in 597, Hume wrote, 'as their ancestors had ever done in their most sanguinary triumphs, and most splendid victories'.[48] He showed how these early spiritual conquerors had preyed on the credulity and superstition of a barbarous people, how they had gained ascendancy over the Saxon kings and, Hume commented, their wives;[49] how they had acquired lands and privileges. During the

Norman era, the priests had behaved as feudal barons who had their own ways of checking royal power when it suited them, as Henry II had discovered in his dealings with Becket and King John discovered to his cost at the time of the Magna Carta. They had been capable of mobilizing the whole apparatus of feudal military power to wage a holy war to recover Jerusalem from the Turks, 'the most signal and most durable monument of human folly, that has yet appeared in any age or nation'.[50] In that terrible era in which the feudal system declined into barbarism and civil war, the Church alone had prevented the total collapse of society.

> Though the religion of that age can merit no better name than that of superstition, it served to unite together a body of men who had great sway over the people, and who kept the community from falling to pieces, by the factions and independent power of the nobles. And what was of great importance; it threw a mighty authority into the hands of men, who by their profession were averse to arms and violence; who tempered by their mediation the general disposition towards military enterprizes; and who still maintained, even amidst the shock of arms, those secret links, without which it is impossible for human society to subsist.[51]

Hume's *longue durée* had shown that England's early history had been locked into a feudal system whose social fabric and whose political and religious institutions had been utterly destroyed by the Tudor era. He had shown that absolute royal authority, helped by the civilizing power of luxury and commerce, had seemed to be the only force capable of turning England into a civilized society. The problem with which Hume left his readers was whether the limited monarchy which had been brought into existence in the seventeenth century would be capable of serving the same ends in a world which was being transformed by commerce. He ended with a moral distilled from his understanding of philosophy and of the politics and history of England.

> In each of these successive alterations, the only rule of government, which is intelligible or carries any authority with it, is the established practice of the age, and the maxims of administration, which are at that

time prevalent, and universally assented to. Those who, from a pretended respect to antiquity, appeal at every turn to an original plan of the constitution, only cover their turbulent spirit and their private ambition under the appearance of venerable forms; and whatever period they pitch on for their model, they may still be carried back to a more ancient period, where they will find the measures of power entirely different, and where every circumstance, by reason of the greater barbarity of the times, will appear still less worthy of imitation. Above all, a civilized nation, like the English, who have happily established the most perfect and most accurate system of liberty that was ever found compatible with government, ought to be cautious in appealing to the practice of their ancestors, or regarding the maxims of uncultivated ages as certain rules for their present conduct. An acquaintance with the ancient periods of their government is chiefly *useful* by instructing them to cherish their present constitution, from a comparison or contrast with the condition of those distant times. And it is also *curious* by shewing them the remote, and commonly faint and disfigured originals of the most finished and most noble institutions, and by instructing them in the great mixture of accident, which commonly concurs with a small ingredient of wisdom and foresight, in erecting the complicated fabric of the most perfect government.[52]

7

Philosophy, History and *The History of England*

With the publication of the two volumes of 'Antient History' in 1762, Hume's work as a historian had entered its final phase. Although he now had the text of a history of England from the Roman invasion to the Revolution of 1688, the question of whether or not to complete it with a volume on the reigns of William III and Queen Anne was still unresolved. Nor was he wholly satisfied with the existing text and was to spend a remarkable amount of time in the last fourteen years of his life correcting and polishing it.

The question of the further volume continued to vex Hume until 1768. The attractions of going forward in time were obvious. His publishers and friends continued to urge him to carry on. Access to the Royal Archives was arranged, 'all imaginable assistance' was offered, and on 6 October 1766 Hume got as far as promising to 'Sketch out the Outlines of the two or three subsequent Reigns' for his publisher. By 1768, however, the mood had changed. 'I believe . . . I shall write no more history,' he told his friend William Mure, repeating the same message to his publisher on 22 May 1770. 'I am fully determined never to continue my History, and have indeed put it entirely out of my power by retiring to this Country [Scotland] for the rest of my Life.'[1] This was not entirely surprising. The six published volumes were already making Hume a rich man: by the end of his life they would have made at least £4–5,000.[2] More seriously, he had every reason to be apprehensive about the reception a new volume would receive. Ever optimistic about the reception of his works, he had been taken aback and discouraged by the reception of his history of the Stuarts.[3] It was plain that if this had been capable of generating such an uproar, the history of a more recent political world, riven by bitter party disputes over the Revolution, the Succession, the Church and the wars with France would be even more likely to plunge Hume into deep controversial waters. Nor can it have been a coincidence that Hume's interest in writing a final volume should have evaporated during a confused, turbulent and, for him, distressing, period of political history.

The accession of George III in 1760 had witnessed the disintegration of the party system he had known in the 1740s when working on the *Essays Moral, Political and Literary*. Parties and political groupings had fragmented, governments had become perilously short-lived and unstable. An increasingly vociferous press had ensured that wild assertions that the King was attempting to create a new Stuart Despotism by installing a Scot, the Earl of Bute, as Prime Minister, had spilled over from parliament into the streets of London and the English constituencies, fuelling what Hume felt was a dismaying and often Scotophobic eruption of popular demagoguery and protest, an apparent reversion to the politics of an earlier age which seemed to threaten the very existence of the constitution. The cry of the 'factious Barbarians' of London, that liberty was in danger, 'exceeds the Absurdity of Titus Oates and the popish Plot', Hume wrote, wondering whether it was possible that 'the popular Discontent may not reach the Army, who have a pretence for Discontents of their own?' It seemed to him that the response of government to a mob crying up liberty in danger had been so uncertain that there was now a danger of government itself becoming 'an absolute Chimera: so much Liberty is incompatible with human Society: and it will be happy if we can escape from it, without falling into a military Government, such as Algiers or Tunis'.[4] Indeed it was a crisis which seemed to call into question every optimistic enlightened assumption that the progress of civilization was irreversible. In June 1768, in one of his calmer moments, he repeated the awful fear that the English constitution was more likely to turn into a military despotism than into the benign species of absolute monarchy which he had invoked in the *Essays*. As he put it in a letter to a French friend.

> Pray, do not the late Events in this Country appear a little contrary to your System? Here is a people thrown into Disorders (not dangerous

ones I hope) merely from the Abuse of Liberty, chiefly the Liberty of the Press: without any Grievance, I do not only say, real, but even imaginary; and without any of them being able to tell one Circumstance of Government which they wish to have corrected: They roar Liberty, tho' they have apparently more Liberty than any people in the World; a great deal more than they deserve: and perhaps more than any men ought to have. The same perfection of our Government, carried to an Extreme, has a bad influence on our Ministers: There is too little difference between the Governors and Governed. A Minister here can amass no Fortune, being checked in every Abuse: he can very little give Employments to his own Friends, Favourites and Flatterers, but must bestow all Offices on those who by their Votes and Credit may support Government; and he can revenge himself on none of his Enemies; because every one is so entrenched in Laws and privileges, as to be able to set all the World at Defiance. Hence men of great Rank and Fortune are very indifferent about being Ministers; being sensible, that they are more exposed to Obloquy on account of their power, and derive no consideration from it. They either decline high Offices, or behave negligently in them: and express every moment their Wishes of being free of the Trouble and Subjection, attending them. These Sentiments loosen the Attachment of their Inferiors.[5]

Under these circumstances, he told Andrew Millar, and given the Scotophobia of the London mob, 'I dread, if I shou'd undertake a more modern History, the Impertinence & Ill-manners, to which it wou'd expose me.'[6]

For Hume English political folly made it all the more important that the existing volumes of the history should be revised so as to convey his historical messages as accurately, clearly and readably as possible, and it was for this reason that he was to commit himself to a process of revision which had begun with the publication of the first Stuart volume and was to continue for the rest of his life. He was always receptive to criticism on matters of fact, even when it came from the hostile pen of 'a mangy cur' like William Tytler, a Scottish Minister who had written a long pamphlet to traduce his treatment of the Marian Controversy.[7] Stylistic corrections were equally welcome, particularly those which involved purging his text of Scotticisms which would annoy fastidious

English readers.[8] But serious revision meant smoothing out the narrative of a history that would now be read chronologically and above all, vindicating his claim to be an 'impartial' historian. The first problem was easily solved. With the publication of the two Tudor volumes, Hume was able to consign most of the digressions on the Tudor monarchy and the effects of the Reformation which had interrupted the narrative of the first Stuart volume to notes and appendices. The publication of the Tudor volumes had also provoked the important criticism from Horace Walpole that Hume had failed to cite his authorities. Hume replied that his narrative style was 'rapid' and modelled on 'the concise manner of the ancient Historians' and on moderns like Machiavelli and Paolo Sarpi.[9] However, he admitted that he had overlooked the modern taste for citing authorities. 'And, tho' it be easy for the falsest and most partial historian to load his margin with quotations, nor is there any other certain method of assuring ones self of the fidelity of an author than to read most of the original writers of any period: yet the reader has reason to expect that the most material facts, at least all such as are in any way new, should be supported by the proper authorities.'[10] The business of adding references proved to be more demanding than Hume had anticipated. He told his publisher that 'I find myself oblig'd to read over again almost all my old Authors: & besides adding the References, I take an Opportunity to correct a few Mistakes, to add some new Facts & to make Improvements on the whole. I fancy I shall be able to put my Account of the Period of English History beyond Controversy.'[11] As an author who wrote very quickly – the two volumes of Tudor history were written between the spring of 1757 and the summer of 1758 – Hume seemed to be admitting that his narrative had sometimes become distanced from his sources. One of the most important purposes of his revisions was to close this gap and to acknowledge the authority which citation gave to his narrative.

Hume's revisions were also motivated by his need to vindicate his claim to be an 'impartial' historian. As a friendly critic, Owen Ruffhead, pointed out, the trouble was that many readers found Hume's judgements 'singular' or 'eccentric' rather than impartial:

> It is but just to acknowledge, that the historian, in recounting the revolutions of this period has, upon the whole, proceeded with great

freedom of inquiry, and impartiality of judgement. He has occasionally done justice to all sects, and all parties: he does not appear to be in the least tinctured with that bigotry, which disposes men to adopt particular received tenets and opinions in religion and politics. But though he is free from all slavish zeal for the systems of others, he is not exempt from a frailty scarce less dangerous, which is a passion for singularity.[12]

Hume seems to have been prepared to accept that his religious views would appear 'singular' to most of his readers. However, his political views, and more particularly 'the plaguy Prejudices of Whiggism, with which I was too much infected when I began this Work', were another matter. These 'plaguy prejudices' about the royal prerogative, the constitutional position of the House of Commons and the libertarian instincts of those who had opposed royal government at different periods of history were, he admitted, difficult to control. He told Sir Gilbert Elliot in 1763. 'I corrected some of these Mistakes in a former Edition: but being resolv'd to add to this Edition the Quotations & Authorities for the Reigns of James I & Charles I, I was oblig'd to run over again the most considerable Authors who had treated of these Reigns. I now find that they above all the rest, have been corrupted with Whig Rancour, & that I really deserv'd the name of a Party Writer, and boasted without any Foundation of my Impartiality.'[13] As a 'sceptical whig', the problem of rooting out these deeply seated prejudices was to preoccupy him for the rest of his life.

Hume's narrative of events, distilled from published chronicles and histories known to his contemporaries, remained his most universally admired achievement. Meticulously corrected in editions published between 1762 and 1778, it was a narrative written in the hope that it would entertain and instruct impartially minded readers, whatever their religious or political persuasions, and would prompt them to discuss the author's judgements even when they seemed to be at odds with more conventional orthodoxies. As to the charge that these judgements were idiosyncratic rather than impartial, Hume was able to reply that his rationale could be found in the strategically placed appendices which discussed the principles of government and the state of the economy and manners at different periods of English history. As Owen Ruffhead commented, these appendices were more likely to attract the studious rather than the general reader. Nevertheless, they ensured that 'the attentive Reader will find that philosophy and jurisprudence constantly go hand in hand with History' and, as another reviewer put it, ensured that Hume himself would appear 'not only the philosopher and politician, but in many instances the orator' who was inviting his readers to exercise the same sort of Spectatorial impartiality Addison had recommended his readers use in reflecting on the manners and morals of the modern world.[14] The ultimate paradox which the *History* exposed was that it was just as hard to turn oneself into an impartial spectator of England's past history as it was to become an impartial spectator of its present.

Once completed, the *History of England* became an instant best-seller. Five editions of the completed work appeared between 1762 and Hume's death in 1776. Fifty more appeared in the next fifty years. It was translated into French, German, Spanish and Dutch and republished in America. There were abridgements for students, and little pocket editions charmingly and sentimentally illustrated and probably designed for ladies. There were selections of Hume's 'Characters' of England's kings, queens and statesmen for those who were interested in Hume's views of prudential statesmanship. There was even an edition 'revised for family use with such omissions and alterations as may render it salutory to the young and unexceptionable to the Christian'. Above all, there were editions published with Tobias Smollett's *From the Revolution to the Death of George II (designed as a continuation of Mr Hume)* in five volumes and first published in 1763–5.

Hume's immense readership suggests that he had, at last, succeeded in doing what he had always wanted by bringing his interests in the principles of human nature, the progress of civilization and the political culture of contemporary Britain into focus in a way which the polite world could understand and on terms to which historians would have to respond in the future. It was not easy for antiquaries or the ever-inventive disciples of Mary Queen of Scots to dislodge his reasoning about the Saxon constitution or the Marian Controversy with new facts, although inevitably and significantly more damage could be inflicted on his account of recent history by new archival discoveries. For Hume's historical reasoning is so cogent and so carefully regulated by philosophical distinctions that it soon became clear that revising his revisionism would be a matter of attacking philosophical premises rather than historical facts. Clerics and Whigs soon realized that the devastation he had visited on religion and ideas of liberty was the result of a theory of opinion which would have to be rebutted by showing that not all forms of knowledge were as wayward as Hume had supposed. Clerical historians called on theology to show that the authority of true religion and the course of its history had been determined by the Deity and could not be explained in terms of priestcraft. Whigs like John Millar, the Scottish jurist and historian who understood Hume too well to be able to answer him effectively, tried to show that property had a much greater power to shape mankind's opinions than Hume had supposed. The brisk, formidable Whig blue-stocking, Catharine Macaulay, simply cut the Gordian knot by protesting that the constitution was the work of patriots and providence, not of mere mortals who had never risen above 'the stamp of vulgar life'.[15] Not enough is known about the shift in popular British historical culture that took place in the half-century following the appearance of the *History of England*. But, if it is true that revolutions in historical understanding involve rethinking the principles of human nature, as well as the facts of history, Hume's *History* may well turn out to be one of the few genuinely revolutionary histories of England.

By the middle of the nineteenth century, the popularity of the *History* was on the wane, displaced by the neo-Whig history of T. B. Macaulay, which appeared between 1849 and 1861. It too was history on an epic scale, designed to reconstruct the Whig view of history in the wake of the devastation which Hume had visited on it. Macaulay wanted to re-establish the continuties in English history that Hume had undermined, by showing that England's political institutions were more ancient, better constructed and more durable than he had imagined, and that Englishmen had possessed loftier views of liberty than Hume had allowed. It was a thicker-crusted account of English civilization. Hume's long day was over. By the mid-1890s the *History* went out of print for the first time and remained so until 1983, neglected by philosophers and historians alike. It is not difficult to see why this should have been so. The *History* was deeply rooted in the polemical world of early-eighteenth-century historiography and in the controversies of historians whose credibility Hume had devastated. No one except specialists reads any of these historians now, and one of Hume's most decisive achievements was to convince posterity that it had no reason to do otherwise. In that respect, at least, Hume was the author of his own neglect.

And this is a pity, for Hume's achievement as a historian was remarkable. His concerns with philosophy, politeness and prudence had yielded the first genuinely political history of England. The history of civilization in England could no longer be told in terms of the fortunes of an ancient constitution. It was now the story of a nation whose people's political behaviour had been shaped by laws and customs, by property, religion and culture, and by the securities and insecurities of the ages in which they lived. It was the story of an all too often broken line of kings, who had seized or inherited their thrones and were faced with the daily problems of survival in worlds which were populated by pretenders, politicians and prelates, who were forever attempting to manipulate the people's ideas of their interests and attempting to challenge and undermine royal authority. No historian before or since has had so subtle and powerful a sense of the interests that shape the political behaviour of mankind, and few have had a sharper insight into the ever-changing character of the political prudence that was needed to manipulate it.

All of this establishes Hume as a fine historian. But what establishes his claim to greatness is his insistence that the history of civilization must begin and end with politics. The unique capacity of human beings to create and obey governments was the key to the civilizing process, the key that had the power to unlock a people's capacity for justice, humanity and wisdom. Then, and only then, could mankind hope to enjoy what visionaries and constitutionalists had always longed for – societies which were governed by laws, not men, societies which were secure against the vicissitudes of incompetence and ill-fortune.

No historian of Britain has made a stronger plea for the history of civilization as political history, and no one could have pleaded less dogmatically than Hume. His history is discursive in the sense that it is designed to generate conversation and reflection among his readers and to encourage them to engage in the delightful business of passing judgement on those who have shaped past events and those who have written about them. This is a long way from the high Germanic ideal of history as science and it is far more modest as well. Believing that history is a science means believing in a past which exists independently of the historian and is recoverable by him. It means believing in the possibility of authoritative history and in historians who are able to legislate for their readers. But Hume's discursive philosophical history is not in the least authoritative. It is written for those who are curious about their past, and want to rethink the stories they have been told about the worlds they have lost. He sets agendas for those who want to discuss the past seriously; he provides the data and sets the contexts in which great events took place; he provides intellectual tools which are worthy of intelligent people; and invites his readers to exercise their own judgements about the significance of these events in their own ways and in their own time. There is nothing in the *History* and nothing in Hume's philosophy to allow him to legislate historiographically for his readers.

And this from the man who saw in philosophical history the framework out of which a science of man could be constructed. The primary purpose of that science of man had been to release human beings from Christian bondage and to provide them with a model of themselves as historical agents whose understanding of themselves, their interests and their happiness was shaped in the time-bound, historical world of common life; theology was to be dethroned in favour of philosophical history. But Hume had no intention of paving the way for a new clerisy of historians with new and mystical canons of historical truth to tease and perplex the understanding. Indeed, one of the main purposes of the *History of England* had been to dash the pretensions of party historians who were in danger of establishing a tyranny over the opinions of modern Britons which was every bit as insidious as that of the priests. Only by teaching men and women to reflect historically on the processes by which they had acquired an understanding of the world, only by showing them how the culture in which they had been inducted had been formed; only thus could human beings be shown how to distance themselves from their past and devote themselves to the peaceful pursuit of their interests in the material world in which they found themselves. For it was as important for the philosophical historian to liberate human beings from the priestcraft of historians as it was to liberate them from the clerics.

Notes and Bibliography

The following abbreviations have been used:

THN: David Hume. *A Treatise of Human Nature*, ed. L. A. Selby-Bigge, second edition revised by P. H. Nidditch (Oxford, 1978).

Essays: David Hume. *Essays Moral, Political and Literary*, ed. Eugene F. Miller (Indianapolis, 1985).

Dialogues: *Hume's Dialogues Concerning Natural Religion*, ed. N. Kemp Smith, second edition (London, 1947).

Enquiries: David Hume. *Enquiries Concerning Human Understanding and Concerning the Principles of Morals*, ed. L. A. Selby-Bigge and P. H. Nidditch (Oxford, 1975).

HE: David Hume. *The History of England from the Invasion of Julius Caesar to the Revolution in 1688*, 6 vols., ed. W. B. Todd (Indianapolis. 1983).

HL: *The Letters of David Hume*, ed. J. Y. T. Grieg, 2 vols. (Oxford, 1969).

NHL: *New Letters of David Hume*, ed. R. Klibansky and E. C. Mossner (Oxford, 1954).

Mossner: E. C. Mossner, *The Life of David Hume* (Oxford, 1970).

Prologue

1. HL i, 33.
2. THN, xvi.
3. Mossner, 582; HL, i, 158.

1. Life and Letters

1. The definitive text of Hume's autobiographical essay, 'My own Life', is to be found in Mossner's *Life*, Appendix A, 611–15.

2. 'Hume at La Fleche, 1735: An Unpublished Letter', ed. E. C. Mossner, *Texas Studies in English*, xxxvii, 1958, 30–33.

3. R. Mudie, *The Modern Athens: A Dissection and Demonstration of Men and Things in the Scotch Capital* (London, 1825), 162.

4. *A Letter from a Gentlemen in the Country to his Friend in the City With an Answer thereto concerning the New Edinburgh Assembly* (Edinburgh, 1723).

5. THN, 264.

6. Mossner, 66.

7. Mossner, 612.

8. E. C. Mossner, 'Hume as Literary Patron: A Suppressed Review of Robert Henry's History of Great Britain 1773', *Modern Philology*, 1942, 361–82.

9. Mossner, 302.

10. Mossner, 613.

11. Mossner, 443.

12. Mossner, 504.

13. My thanks to Alexander Murdoch for this reference.

14. [James Boswell,] *Boswell in Extremes*, 1776–1778, ed. C. M. Weis and F. A. Pottle (New York, 1970), 11–15.

Bibliographical Note

Mossner remains the indispensable but dated introductory guide to Hume's life. It is not helpful on the all-important matter of the religious environment in which Hume grew up, and suffers, like most eighteenth-century Scottish history, from the absence of serious work on the history of Scottish Presbyterianism before the establishment of the moderate regime in 1752. Orthodox Presbyterianism is a more complex phenomenon than Mossner allows and more theologically sophisticated too, as Hume's portrait of the orthodox Christian, Demea, one of the main protagonists in the *Dialogues*, suggests. R. B. Sher's *Church and University in the Scottish Enlightenment* (Edinburgh, 1985) is essential reading for the history of the Kirk after 1752, and on Hume's relations with it. Mossner's *Life* was written before the present interest in the history of the Scottish Enlightenment had taken shape. There is much exciting research on the way into the cultural and intellectual contexts in which Hume grew up, notably in relation to the changes which were taking place in the Scottish universities in the early decades of the century and into the relationship between moral, natural and medical philosophy. On these, see the bibliographical note to Chapter 3. A future biography is likely to present Hume as a man who grew up in a more intricate and fluid religious, political and intellectual environment than that to which we have become accustomed. He will certainly appear as someone who struggled long, hard and largely unsuccessfully to establish a professional toe-hold within it. A preliminary glimmering of a more frustrated Hume appears in V. Wexler, *David Hume and the History of England* (Philadelphia, 1979). And he will undoubtedly appear as a man of letters who was deeply preoccupied with the role of learning and letters in a modern polity. On this, see J. Christensen, *Practicing Enlightenment: Hume and the Formation of a Literary Career* (Madison, Wisc., 1987). But the final test of the adequacy of a future biography will continue to be its ability to chart Hume's classic escape from the confines of Christian culture and his influence on Scottish and English intellectual culture. Peter Gay, *The Enlightenment: An Interpretation* (2 vols., New York, 1966 and 1969) is still the most thought-provoking study of the wider context for such a study. Charles Camic, *Experience and Enlightenment: Socialization for Cultural Change in Eighteenth-Century Scotland* (Edinburgh, 1983) is an intelligent, sociologically sophisticated reminder that the intellectual preoccupations of the Scottish Enlightenment, like those of its greatest philosopher and historian, were constantly and centrally concerned with religion.

2. Politics, Politeness and Men of Letters

1. J. A. W. Gunn, *Factions No More: Attitudes to Party in Government and Opposition in Eighteenth-Century England* (London, 1972) is a useful introduction to the subject.
2. C. Leslie, *Rehearsals*, no. 14, 4 Nov. 1704. I am grateful to Paul Monod for this reference.
3. Notably, E. Cruickshanks, *Political Untouchables* (London, 1979); L. Colley, *In Defiance of Oligarchy: The Tory Party 1714–60* (Cambridge,

1982); and J. C. D. Clark, *English Society 1688–1832* (Cambridge, 1985).

4. J. H. Plumb, *The Growth of Political Stability in England, 1660–1730* (London, 1967) and P. M. G. Dickson, *The Financial Revolution in England: A Study in the Development of Public Credit* (London, 1967) did most to open up this line of enquiry.

5. J. G. A. Pocock's 'The Varieties of Whiggism from Exclusion to Reform: A History of Ideology and Discourse' in his *Virtue, Commerce, and History: Essays on Political Thought and History, chiefly in the Eighteenth Century* (Cambridge, 1985), 215–310, is an important recent attempt at synthesizing the history of Whig political thought.

6. I am grateful to J. A. W. Gunn for this reference.

7. John, Baron Hervey, *Ancient and Modern Liberty Stated and Compar'd* (London, 1734), 61–2.

8. Ibid., 5.

9. J. Black, *The British Press in the Age of Walpole* (London, 1984). M. Harris, 'Publishing, Print and Politics in the Age of Walpole' in *Britain in the Age of Walpole*, ed. J. Black (London, 1984), 196.

10. 'Of the Liberty of the Press', *Essays*, 11–12.

11. Politeness has only recently begun to interest students of early-eighteenth-century political thought. For a useful introduction see Pocock, 'Varieties of Whiggism', and my 'Politics and Politeness in the Reigns of Anne and the Early Hanoverians' in *The Varieties of British Political Thought*, ed. J. G. A. Pocock (Cambridge, 1993), 211–45. See also L. Klein, *Shaftesbury and the Culture of Politeness* (Cambridge. 1994).

12. 'The True-Born Englishman'. Defoe's writings anticipate the modern Whiggery of the Walpolian era. See for example *Some Reflections on a Pamphlet lately Publish'd entitled, An Argument Shewing that a standing Army is inconsistent with Free Government* (2nd edn, London, 1697).

13. D. Defoe, *A Tour through the Whole Island of Great Britain*, Preface to vol. 1. The abridged edition (Harmondsworth, 1986) has a useful introduction by Pat Rogers.

14. D. F. Bond's edition of *The Spectator* (Oxford, 1965) is indispensable. The essays are numbered consecutively and identically in every edition and I cite them accordingly.

15. *Spectator*, nos. 167, 201, 447.

16. Ibid., no. 324.

17. J. Addison, *The Freeholder*, ed. J. Leheny (Oxford, 1979), 192.

18. Quoted by W. Ferguson, *Scotland, 1689 to the Present* (Edinburgh, 1968), 34.

19. In what follows, I have relied heavily on my own work on the origin of the Scottish Englightement. It is summarized in 'The Scottish Enlightenment' in *The Enlightenment in National Contexts*, ed. R. Porter and M. Teich (Cambridge, 1981) and in 'Politics, Politeness, and the Anglicisation of Early Eighteenth-Century Scottish Culture' in *Scotland and England 1286–1815*, ed. R. A. Mason (Edinburgh, 1987), 226–46.
20. *Edinburgh Review* (Edinburgh, 1755–6), Preface.
21. 'Of Refinement in the Arts', *Essays*, 277–8.
22. Ibid., 280–81.

Bibliographical Note

The political history of Britain from the Glorious Revolution to 1760 is being radically reconstructed. The work of Plumb and Dickson cited above brought into focus the importance of the growth of the executive and the role of patronage and public credit in shaping post-revolution politics. J. G. A. Pocock, *The Machiavellian Moment: Florentine Political Thought and the Atlantic Republican Tradition* (Princeton, 1975 laid the foundations for all subsequent attempts to establish the ideological contexts within which the political culture of the early eighteenth century developed. How far this story can be told in terms of the growth of political stability and the elimination of party politics is now highly dubious. The works cited in note 3 provide conclusive evidence that Tory politics and Tory political culture survived the rise of Walpole, provoking important questions about the nature and significance of opposition politics, about the relationship between Toryism and Jacobitism and about Bolingbroke's attempts to build a new country party. Pocock's *Machiavellian Moment* and H. T. Dickinson, *Liberty and Property: Political Ideology in Eighteenth-Century Britain* (London, 1977) stress the significance of court–country tensions in early-eighteenth-century party politics, place considerable weight on the highly intellectualized opposition Whiggery at the expense of more ancient and primitive distrust of courts and loyalties to county communities. They also underestimate the religious component of Tory ideology and its importance in underpinning powerful ideological commitments to ideas of the divine and indefeasible rights of the Stuart dynasty, something that, it is interesting to note, Hume took very seriously indeed. On this see particularly Clark's *English Society* cited above and Paul Monod, 'Jacobitism and Country Principles in the Reign of William iii', *Historical Journal*, 30 (1987), 289–310. On the intricate history of Whiggery and the sophisticated thought of opposition Whigs reared in a republican tradition which Hume deeply distrusted, see Dickinson, *Liberty and Property*, and Pocock's fascinating review of his own earlier account of the ideological geography of the period in 'Varieties of Whiggery' cited above. Politeness, both in the age of Defoe and Addison and later in the age of Walpole, has not yet been adequately researched or built into the revisionist picture of early-eighteenth-century politics. Pocock's 'Varieties of Whiggery' summarizes the present state of play. Lawrence Klein, *Shaftesbury and the Culture of Politeness* (Cambridge, 1994) opens the subject up. My 'Politics and Politeness' develops the argument presented here. M. B. Ketcham, *Transparent Designs: Reading, Performance and Form in the 'Spectator'* (Athens, Ga, 1985) at least treats Addison with the seriousness he deserves. I have written about the lofty pretensions of Scottish politeness in the essays cited above. Politeness has attracted the attention of modern sociologists. E. Goffman, *Interaction Ritual: Essays on Face to Face Behavior* (New York, 1967) and P. Brown and S. C. Levinson, *Politeness: Some Universals in Language Usage* (Cambridge, 1987) may be read as the work of latter-day Addisonians.

3. Scepticism, Science and the Natural History of Man

1. NHL, 26.
2. *Boswell in Extremes*, 11.
3. Quoted in R. Popkin, *The History of Scepticism from Erasmus to Spinoza* (Berkeley, Los Angeles and London, 1979), 31.
4. *Dialogues*, 132.
5. *Spectator*, no. 37.
6. *Malebranche's Search after Truth: or a Treatise of the Nature of the Humane Mind, and of its Management for Avoiding Error in the Sciences*, trans. R. Sault (London, 1694), Preface.
7. Ibid.

8. Religious scepticism in Scotland is an unstudied subject. The following sources, all of which were in circulation when Hume was a boy, show that there is a subject waiting to be opened up. *An Apology for Mr Thomas Rhind, or An Account of the manner how, and the reasons for which he separated from the Presbyterian party and embraced the communion of the [Episcopalian] Church* (Edinburgh, 1712) is the work of a Presbyterian who used an elementary from of scepticism to dislodge his strict Presbyterian faith and turn himself into some sort of Episcopalian. T. Halyburton's *Memoirs* (Edinburgh, 1714) with subsequent editions in 1715, 1718, 1733; and J. Anderson's *A Defence of the Church, Government, Faith, Worship and Spirit of the Presbyterians* (Edinburgh, 1714) are the work of well-known, heavyweight orthodox Presbyterians who were perfectly familiar with the fideistic potential of scepticism.

9. C. MacLaurin, *An Account of Sir Isaac Newton's Philosophical Discoveries* (2nd edn, London, 1750), 396.

10. F. Hutcheson, *An Essay on the Nature and Conduct of the Passions and Affections* (London, 1972), xvii.

11. THN, Introduction, xvii, xix.

12. *Dialogues*, 139.

13. HL, i, 154.

14. Ibid.

15. THN, 182–3.

16. THN, 180.

17. THN, 207.

18. THN, 252.

19. THN, 225.

20. THN, 68.

21. THN, 268–9.

22. THN, 316.

23. THN, 363.

24. THN, 534. Cf. *Enquiries*, 188.

25. THN, 486–9.

26. THN, 490.

27. *Enquiries*, 306. Cf. THN, 490.

28. THN, 558.

29. *Enquiries*, 194.

Bibliographical Note

The literature on the *Treatise* is vast and mostly designed to set Hume's work in different philosophical contexts. The following deal in different ways with Hume's philosophical development and will be helpful to those who want to link his philosophical writing to his writing on politics and history. On scepticism generally, see Popkin's *History of Scepticism* cited above and *The Sceptical Tradition*, ed. M. Burnyeat (Berkeley, Los Angeles and London, 1983). On Hume's extremely complex critique of the various scepticisms available to him – a subject I have not begun to tackle in this chapter – see R. Popkin's classic 'David Hume: His Pyrrhonism and his Critique of Pyrrhonism' in *Hume*, ed. V. C. Chappell (New York, 1966) and R. J. Fogelin, *Hume's Scepticism in the Treatise of Human Nature* (London, 1985). The history of religious scepticism in Scotland badly needs attention, but see note 8 to Chapter 3 above. The natural and medical scientific contexts for Hume's thought is attracting attention, though the time is not yet ripe for synthesis. See J. P. Wright, *The Sceptical Realism of David Hume* (Manchester, 1983) and M. M. Barfoot, in *Hume and the Culture of Science in Early-Eighteenth-Century Britain* (Oxford, 1989). On Hume's theory of the passions, see P. Ardal, *Passion and Value in Hume's Treatise* (Edinburgh, 1966). On the classical affiliations of his theory of the sentiments, see useful suggestions in P. Jones, *Hume's Sentiments: Their Ciceronian and French Context* (Edinburgh, 1982). A. C. Baier, *A Progress of Sentiments. Reflections on Hume's* Treatise (Cambridge, Mass., 1991), is suggestive and important. Duncan Forbes, *Hume's Philosophical Politics* (Cambridge, 1975) and Knut Haakonssen, *The Science of a Legislator: The Natural Jurisprudence of David Hume and Adam Smith* (Cambridge, 1981) set Hume in the context of the complex contemporary debate about the principles of natural jurisprudence. D. Miller, *Philosophy and Ideology in Hume's Political Thought* (Oxford, 1982) is a sensible introduction to his political thought. J. Robertson's *The Scottish Enlightenment and the Militia Issue* (Edinburgh, 1985) relates Hume's political thought to Scottish preoccupations with the classical republican tradition. More generally, the role of reason in Hume's understanding of human nature has recently attracted much scholarly attention. Traditional ideas that Hume was a naturalist have been decisively disposed of by D. Fate Norton's *David Hume: Common-Sense Moralist, Sceptical Metaphysician* (Princeton, 1982), which also provides an absorbing discussion of Hume's moral theory in its contemporary context. Hume's discussion of the manner in which we enter into conventions to establish a moral and political culture lies at the heart of questions about the nature of rationality in Hume's thought. Here his understanding of language and politeness is of crucial importance, and is a matter to which I do not think that historians of philosophy have paid enough attention. Nor, in my view, and in my discussion in this book, do I believe that they have fully understood the crucial importance of custom and habit in shaping our understanding, a matter which becomes much clearer in the *History of England*. On Hume as a polite man of letters, J. Christensen's *Practising Enlightenment* is suggestive. Overall, D. W. Livingston's *Hume's Philosophy of Common Life* (Chicago and London, 1984) can be recommended as by far the most thoughtful and pregnant modern attempt to make sense of Hume's philosophical development: it is strongest on his metaphysics, less so on his political and historical writing.

4. A Philosopher's Agenda for a History of England

1. Mossner, 138.
2. 'Advertisement'. Not republished in modern editions and to be found in *Essays, Moral and Political* (Edinburgh, 1741), iii–v.
3. HL, ii, 257.
4. 'Of Essay Writing', *Essays*, 534–5.
5. 'Of the Delicacy of Taste and Passion', *Essays*, 7–8.
6. 'Of Essay Writing', *Essays*, 567–8; 'Of the Middle Station of Life', *Essays*, 546–9.
7. *The works of Lord Bolingbroke*, 4 vols. (Philadelphia, 1841: reprinted 1969), Vol. 2, Letter xiii, 117.
8. Ibid., Letter i, 27.
9. Ibid., Letter xii, 115.
10. Ibid., Letter ii, 30.
11. Ibid., Letter iv, 48; Letter vii, 71.
12. Ibid., Letter x, 95.

13. 'That Politics may be Reduced to a Science', *Essays*, 25–7.
14. 'Whether the British Government inclines more to Absolute Monarchy or to a Republic', *Essays*, 51. 'Of the First Principles of Government', *Essays*, 32–3.
15. 'Of the First Principles of Government', *Essays*, 33
16. 'Of the Independency of Parliament', *Essays*, 42–5.
17. 'Of Civil Liberty', *Essays*, 94
18. 'Whether the British Government inclines more to Absolute Monarchy or to a Republic', *Essays*, 53.
19. 'Of Parties in General', *Essays*, 54–5.
20. Ibid., 56–7.
21. 'Of the Parties of Great Britain', *Essays*, 64–5.
22. Ibid., 67–70.
23. Ibid., 72.
24. 'Of the Original Contract', *Essays* 466.
25. Ibid., 466.
26. Ibid., 470.
27. Ibid., 472–3.
28. 'Of Superstition and Enthusiasm', *Essays*, 73–5, 78.
29. Ibid., 74, 77–8.
30. 'A Character of Sir Robert Walpole', *Essays*, 5, 4–6. This essay first appeared as the concluding essay to the second volume of essays, published in 1742.

Bibliographical Note

It is impossible to make any sense of Hume's political writing independently of the highly particularized political thought of early-eighteenth-century Britain. Duncan Forbes's *Hume's Philosophical Politics* is a classic, pioneering attempt to take this problem seriously; John Robertson's *The Scottish Enlightenment and the Militia Issue* is helpful and suggestive. David Raynor's introduction to *Sister Peg: A Pamphlet hitherto Unknown by David Hume* (Cambridge, 1982) is an excellent introduction to Hume's political thought which doesn't clinch the case for attributing a pamphlet plausibly attributed to Adam Ferguson to Hume. More work on the political press of the Walpolian era in London and Edinburgh is needed before an exact account of Hume's commentary on contemporary political debate is possible. However, what is clear is that Hume's path through this highly polemical debate was subtle, intricate and surely beyond most of Addison's readers, who had been led to expect essays which could be quickly read and easily digested. On Bolingbroke, see I. Kramnick, *Bolingbroke and his Circle: The Politics of Nostalgia in the Age of Walpole* (London, 1968); H. T. Dickinson, *Bolingbroke* (London, 1970); J. G. A. Pocock, *The Machiavellian Moment*; H. T. Dickinson, *Liberty and Property*, and L. Colley, *In Defiance of Oligarchy*. Quentin Skinner's 'The Principles and Practice of Opposition: The Case of Bolingbroke versus Walpole' in *Historical Perspectives: Studies in English Thought and Society in Honour of J. H. Plumb*, ed. N. McKendrick (London, 1974) is indispensable.

5. *The History of England*: 1

1. J. Addison, *Freeholder*, 194.
2. HL, i, 109.
3. 'Of the Study of History', *Essays*. 567–8.
4. M. Baumstark, 'David Hume: The Making of a Philosophical Historian', Ph.D. thesis. Edinburgh University, 2007, Part 2.
5. HL, i, 170.
6. HL, i, 168.
7. HL, i, 193.
8. HE, vi, 215.
9. P. Rapin de Thoryas. *The History of England*, translated by N. Tindal (2nd edn, 5 vols., London, 1732–51), vol. 2, 160. Rapin is relatively unstudied, but see H. R. Trevor-Roper, 'A Huguenot Historian: Paul Rapin' in *Huguenots in Britain and their French Background. 1550–1800*, ed. I. Scouloudi (London, 1987).
10. P. S. Hicks, *Neo-Classical History and English Culture from Clarendon to Hume* (London, 1996).
11. *The Anecdotes and Egotisms of Henry Mackenzie, 1745–1831*, ed. H. W. Thompson (London. 1927), 169.
12. HE, v, 8, 17.
13. HE, v, 128.
14. HE, v, 39.
15. HE, v, 19.
16. HE, v, 134.

17. Rapin, *History of England*, vol. 2, 155.
18. T. Carte, an Englishman, *A General History of England* (4 vols., London, 1747–55), vol. 3, 703, and vol. 4, 133–4. Carte, like Rapin, has been neglected by historians and deserves much more attention than I have given him here. But see L. Colley, *In Defiance of Oligarchy*, and J. C. D. Clark, *English Society 1688–1832*, for useful background.
19. John, Baron Hervey, *Ancient and Modern Liberty*, 20–29.
20. HE, v, 90, 93.
21. HE, v, 556.
22. HE, v, 93–4.
23. HE, v, 94–5.
24. HE, v, 96.
25. HE, v, 121.
26. HE, v, 159, 160.
27. HE, v, 200.
28. HE, v, 213, 214, 212, 210.
29. HE, v, 217.
30. HE, v, 249–50.
31. HE, v, 223.
32. HE, v, 228.
33. HE, v, 256–7.
34. HE, v, 333.
35. HE, v, 271.
36. HE, v, 297.
37. HE, v, 293, 297–8.
38. HE, v, 304.
39. HE, v, 364.
40. HE, v, 545–6.
41. HE, vi, 141, 3–4, 86, 540.
42. HE, vi, 5.
43. HE, vi, 68–9, 110.
44. HE, vi, 140.
45. HE, vi, 170.
46. HE, vi, 375–6.
47. HE, vi, 376–7.
48. HL, i, 217–18.
49. HE, vi, 307–8.
50. HE, vi, 332–3.
51. HE, vi, 381.
52. HE, vi, 364.

53. This strong statement was included in the first edition but removed from subsequent ones.
54. HE, vi, 469.
55. HE, vi, 496–7.
56. HE, vi, 516–17.
57. HE, vi, 517, 522.
58. HE, vi, 526.
59. HE, vi, 529.
60. HE, vi, 531.
61. HL, i, 240.
62. HE, vi, 377.

Bibliographical Note

G. Giarrizzo's *David Hume, politico e storico* (Turin, 1962) and Duncan Forbes's *Hume's Philosophical Politics* are the only two full-scale attempts to treat Hume as a philosopher turned historian. D. Fate Norton and R. Popkin, *David Hume: Philosophical Historian* (New York, 1965) and V. Wexler, *David Hume and the History of England* (Philadelphia, 1979) are useful and suggestive. But none of these treatments of the *History* fully take stock of the fact that it is, first and foremost, a *political* history which presents politics as the point of entry to the history of civilization and prudence as the point of entry to politics. On this see J. G. A. Pocock, *Barbarism and Religion*, vol. 2, *Narratives of Civil Government* (Cambridge, 1999), section III. See also N. Capaldi and D. W. Livingston, eds., *Liberty in Hume's History of England* (Dordrecht, 1990) and J. A. Herdt, *Religion and Faction in Hume's Moral Philosophy* (Cambridge, 1997). For a view of the *History* which is critical of the one presented here. see D. Wootton, 'David Hume, the Historian', in *The Cambridge Companion to Hume*, ed. D. F. Norton (Cambridge, 1993), 281–312.

6. *The History of England*: 2:
The Tudors and the Early History of England

1. HL, i, 243.
2. HL, i. 249.

3. HE, iii. 134.
4. HE, iii. 76–7.
5. HE, iii, 7, 73.
6. HE, iii, 49.
7. HE, iv, 355.
8. HE, iii, 24.
9. HE, iii, 125, 115.
10. HE, iii, 206–7.
11. HE, iii, 135–6.
12. HE, iii, 139–41.
13. HE, iii, 260.
14. HE, iii, 261, 312, 288.
15. HE, iii, 322–3.
16. HE, iii, 321–2.
17. HE, iii, 338.
18. HE, iii, 441–2.
19. HE, iv, 7–9.
20. HE, iv, 12.
21. HE, iv, 56–7.
22. HE, iv, 119.
23. HE, iv, 41.
24. *The Anecdotes and Egotisms of Henry Mackenzie*, 171.
25. Ibid., 171.
26. HE, iv, 252.
27. HE, iv, 236.
28. HE, iv, 257.
29. HE, iv, 138, 120–1.
30. HE, iv, 122–3.
31. HE, iv, 123.
32. HE, iv, 123–4.
33. HE, iv, 144–5.
34. HE, iv, 178, 180, 145–6.
35. HE, iv, 345–7.
36. HE, iv, 353–4.
37. HL, i, 314.
38. HE, i. 17.
39. HE, i, 297.
40. HE, ii, 311.
41. HE, i, 63, 74.
42. HE, ii, 141.

43. HE, i, 456–7.
44. HE, i, 168–9.
45. HE, ii, 331.
46. HE, ii, 283–4.
47. HE, ii, 109.
48. HE, i, 30.
49. HE, i, 40.
50. HE, i, 234.
51. HE, ii, 4.
52. HE, ii, 525.

7. Philosophy, History and *The History of England*

1. HL, ii, 162, 172, 188, 223.
2. R. B. Sher, *The Enlightenment and the Book* (Chicago, 2006), 241.
3. 'My Own Life', *Essays*, xxxvi–xxxviii.
4. HL, i, 517; ii, 197.
5. HL, ii, 180–1.
6. HL, i, 491.
7. HL, i, 321.
8. HL, i, 233, 236, 369.
9. HL, i, 193, 284.
10. HL, i, 284–5.
11. HL, i, 316–17.
12. *Early Responses to Hume's* History of England, ed. J. Fieser (Bristol, 2003), i, 196.
13. HL, i, 379.
14. *Early Responses*, i, 277, 289, 292.
15. Catherine Macaulay, *The History of England from the Accession of James I to the Revolution*, 8 vols. (London, 1765–71), vol. 7, 493–5.

Bibliographical Note

The subsequent bibliographical history of the *History of England* is best traced in T. E. Jessop. *A Bibliography of David Hume and of Scottish Philosophy from Francis Hutcheson to Lord Balfour* (London, 1938).

Index